"The Future of Connectivity: Unleashing the Power of 5G and Beyond"

"It is important to remember that 5G technology is about more than just speeding up operations; in the long run, low latency and high bandwidth should open up new possibilities for edge computing, extended reality, and the Internet of Things (IoT)". – **Patrick Mukosha**

Table of Contents

Copyright Notice

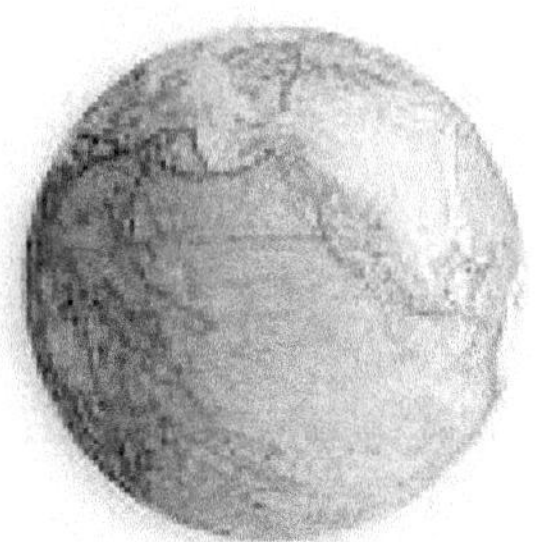

All Rights Reserved.

Trademarks

All terms mentioned in this book that are known to be trademarks or service marks have been appropriately capitalized. The Author and the publisher cannot attest to the accuracy of this information. Use of a term in this book should not be regarded as affecting the validity of any trademark or service mark.

Warning and Disclaimer

Every effort has been made to make this book as complete and as accurate as possible, but no warranty or fitness is implied. The information provided in this book is on as is basis. The Author and the Publisher shall have neither liability nor responsibility to any person or entity with respect to any loss or damage arising from the use the information contained in this book.

Author: Dr. Patrick Chisenga Mukosha

Acknowledgements

The author is indebted to a large number of researchers, and consultants in the field of Information and Communication Technology, whose works were referred to in writing this book – and appears below and in the bibliography.

The author also would like to acknowledge the encouragement of my wife; Gracious Lumba Maboshe-Mukosha, and my children, whose comments and constructive criticism kept the author alive. The author also benefitted from the comments of several of my ICT colleagues. They generously shared their insights and experiences in an evolving field where tacit knowledge is indispensable.

Special thanks go to Lionel Hugh Weston; an Educationalist, British National, my former Secondary School Teacher and Guardian, without whom I would never have had a strong education foundation in life. His contribution in my education career is immeasurable. I shall forever remain indebted to him and the entire Weston's family.

Abstract

"The Future of Connectivity: Unleashing the Power of 5G and Beyond" provides an in-depth analysis of 5G technology and its far-reaching implications across various sectors. This book is designed to offer readers a comprehensive understanding of the technological, economic, and social impacts of 5G, as well as a glimpse into future developments like 6G.

The journey begins with an *exploration of the fundamentals of 5G*, highlighting its advancements over previous generations. Key features such as enhanced speed, reduced latency, and greater capacity are explained, setting the stage for a deeper dive into the technical aspects and potential of 5G.

The book discusses the *crucial components, including small cells, Massive MIMO, and edge computing*. These technologies are critical for achieving the performance benchmarks that make 5G transformative. The book provides detailed case studies and examples of 5G applications in various fields.

5G is the *backbone of the IoT ecosystem*, enabling seamless connectivity across millions of devices. The book explores how 5G facilitates smart homes, smart agriculture, and other IoT applications, driving efficiency and innovation in everyday life and industrial processes.

The book delves into the three core pillars of future mobile communication enabled by 5G: *enhanced mobile broadband (eMBB), ultra-reliable low latency communication (URLLC), and massive machine type communication (mMTC)*. Each pillar is analyzed for its potential to drive technological advancement.

As the world embraces 5G, *the tech industry is already looking ahead to 6G*. The book explores early research and potential applications of 6G, offering insights into what the next generation of connectivity might bring. It discusses the steps necessary to prepare for this future and the innovations that 6G promises.

"The Future of Connectivity: Unleashing the Power of 5G and Beyond" serves as an essential resource for ICT professionals, industry leaders, policymakers, and anyone interested in understanding the transformative power of 5G and the future of global connectivity.

Introduction

The exciting journey of connectivity's evolution is reflected in *the quickening pace of technological advancement and the growing need for more effective and efficient communication in society*. Have you ever considered how far we'll go and how far we've come in terms of connecting with others? I've been thinking a lot about connectedness, and I've always believed that understanding our past may help us better comprehend our present and, more crucially, our potential future directions.

This evolution can be broadly divided into a number of important phases:

(a) **Earlier Modes of Interaction:**

1. **Drumbeats and Smoke Signals:** Ancient societies used drumbeats and smoke signals for *long-distance communication*. Drums were created and used by societies that lived in forests. They were employed for religious and ceremonial purposes, and they were also an early means of long-distance communication.

2. **Couriers and Postal Systems**: In order to *send messages over great distances*, couriers and postal systems were established in ancient empires like Rome and China. The history of postal systems, which are mail or courier services used to transport messages from one location to another, predates the creation of writing and could have been a contributing factor in the development of writing.

(b) **The Phone and Telegraph**:

1. **The Telegraph (1830s–1840s):** Creation of the telegraph (1830s–1840s) *transformed long-distance communication by enabling messages to be conveyed in minutes as opposed to days*. Over a wire constructed between stations, electrical signals were transmitted, revolutionizing long-distance communication. The Telegraph was invented by Samuel Morse (1791-1872) and other inventors.

2. **Telephone (1876):** Real-time voice communication was made possible by *Alexander Graham Bell*'s innovation, which drastically altered both personal and professional communication.

(c) **Wireless Transmission:**

1. **Late 19th And Early 20th Centuries:** Wireless communication was made possible by radio waves, which were essential for use in the military and on ships. *Guglielmo Marconi* invented *Radio.*

2. **Television (1920s–1930s):** This new medium for information and pleasure made visual media widely accessible. The credit for creating the television system goes to a few people. On January 26, 1926, *John Logie Baird* is credited with showing the first live, functional television system in history. Furthermore, *Philo Farnsworth* created the first television system that was entirely electronic. Both had a major influence on the conception and growth of television as we know it today.

(d) **The Internet Era**

1. **Early Networks (1960s–1970s):** ARPANET, the internet's forerunner, proved that international digital communication was feasible. The inception of computer networking can be dated to the early 1960s, when the ARPANET project was started by the US Department of Defense. Building a decentralized communication network that would be immune to a nuclear assault was the aim.

2. **World Wide Web (1990s):** *Tim Berners-Lee*'s creation made the internet a more approachable, accessible medium for communication and information exchange. While employed at CERN in 1989, British scientist Tim Berners-Lee created the World Wide Web (WWW). The necessity for automated information-sharing amongst scientists at universities and institutes around the world led to the initial conception and development of the web.

(e) **Mobile Communication:**

1. **First Generation (1G) (1980s):** Mobile voice communication was made possible via analog cellular networks. The 1980s saw the introduction of 1G, or the initial network generations of mobile networks. These networks were exclusively used for voice conversations and were mostly analog. Following Japan's 1979 introduction of the first 1G network, other nations such as the US and Europe did the same.

2. **Second Generation (2G) (1990s):** The second iteration of mobile telecommunications technology is known as 2G, or second

generation. It made possible the digital transmission of voice and data across cellular networks, displacing the analog 1G technology. Finland hosted the commercial introduction of 2G on the GSM standard in 1991. 1990s saw the introduction of digital voice (such as CDMA – Code Division Multiple Access), digital encryption and SMS (Short Message Service) as part of Second Generation (2G).

3. **Third Generation (3G) (2000s):** Made possible video calls and mobile internet access in the 2000s (such as CDMA2000). The third generation of mobile wireless technology is known as 3G. It is the GSM Evolution networks' upgrading to 2G, 2.5G, GPRS, and 2.75G Enhanced Data Rates, which provides quicker data transfer and higher voice quality. This network was eventually surpassed by 4G and 5G.

4. **Fourth Generation (4G) (2010):** The fourth generation of mobile communication protocols is known as 4G. Comparing its speed and data capacity to that of 3G (Third Generation), it is a major boost. Faster internet speeds, improved voice quality, and compatibility for a variety of apps and services are all goals of 4G networks. The 2010s saw the emergence of Fourth Generation (4G), which significantly boosted data transmission speeds to enable HD video streaming and sophisticated mobile applications. It introduced mobile broadband.

(f) **The Digital Era and Beyond**:

1. **Fifth Generation (5G):** In the 2020s, Fifth Generation (5G) will enable smart cities, driverless cars, and sophisticated robotics by providing ultra-high-speed internet with minimal latency and support for the Internet of Things (IoT). 5G is a more capable and unified air interface. Its expanded capacity allows it to power new deployment models, enable next-generation user experiences, and provide new services. With its fast speeds, excellent dependability, and minuscule latency, 5G will open up new possibilities for the mobile ecosystem. Every business will be impacted by 5G, which will make things like digitalized logistics, remote healthcare, safer transportation, and precision agriculture a reality.

2. **Satellite Internet:** Currently, the only sort of broadband connectivity that residents in remote areas of all 50 states can get is satellite

internet. Satellite internet works by connecting a home internet modem to a satellite in orbit, providing a reliable substitute for anyone without access to DSL, cable, or fiber internet. Businesses like SpaceX's Starlink want to offer high-speed internet connection everywhere, even in isolated places.

3. **Quantum Communication:** This field of study has the potential to completely transform networking once more by offering previously unheard-of speeds and security levels. Data protection using quantum communication makes use of the principles of quantum physics. These rules enable particles to assume a state of superposition, which enables them to concurrently represent many combinations of 1 and 0. For the purpose of transferring data across optical cables, particles are normally photons of light.

(g) Important Technological Advancements:

1. **Fiber Optics:** Developed high-speed, large-capacity networks that revolutionized data transmission. A flexible glass or plastic fiber with the ability to transfer light from one end to the other is called an optical fiber, or optical fiber. These fibers are widely used in fiber-optic communications, which allows data to be transmitted at higher bandwidths (data transfer rates) and over longer distances than electrical lines. Since fibers are resistant to electromagnetic interference and transmit signals with reduced loss, they are utilized in place of metal wires. In addition to being used for illumination, fibers are also utilized for imaging. They are frequently bundled together to enable the usage of fiberscopes, which project images into or out of small areas. Numerous further uses for specially made fibers exist, including fiber optic sensors and fiber lasers.

2. **Wi-Fi:** Without requiring physical connections, wireless local area networks, or WLANs, offer high-speed internet access. Wi-Fi is a wireless technology that transmits data using radio waves. The primary purpose of it is to link gadgets to the internet. Many contemporary electronic gadgets, including computers and cellphones, enable Wi-Fi. Wi-Fi is the signal that a wireless router sends to a device that is close by and has the ability to interpret data.

3. **NFC and Bluetooth**: Are examples of short-range wireless communication technologies that make data sharing and device connectivity easier. Radio waves are used by wireless communication technologies like Bluetooth and NFC to link devices and transfer data. When sending small amounts of data securely across short distances, like for access control and payments, NFC works well. Bluetooth is better suited for wireless devices like speakers and headphones and has a greater connection range.

(h) Effects on the Community

1. **Globalization:** Made international cooperation and trade simpler by facilitating the interconnection of economies, cultures, and people. The process that makes cross-border movement of people and things possible is known as globalization. This economic idea entails the integration of investments, trade, and markets with minimal obstacles preventing the free movement of goods and services across international borders. The term "globalization" also refers to the increasing interconnectedness of the world's economies, cultures, and populations, which is a result of technology, cross-border trade in products and services, investment flows, and information and people movements. Globalization is based on the notion that international openness will increase each country's natural resources.

2. **Social Media:** A social media platform is an online platform that enables users to generate and distribute information, ideas, and material to other individuals or the general public via virtual networks. Users can engage in social networking on social media platforms by leaving comments on other users' work, reposting it, or voicing their opinions. Social media platforms include, but are not limited to, Facebook, Twitter, Instagram, YouTube, TikTok, LinkedIn, and Pinterest.

3. **Remote Work and Education:** Thanks to communication tools and high-speed internet, remote work and education are changing traditional work and learning contexts. Unserved villages can benefit greatly from the presence of remote places, particularly when it comes to remote work and education. By granting access to the

digital world and prospects for economic advancement, technology training has the power to change lives. Schools are attempting to bridge the digital divide, which has shown to be a major obstacle during the pandemic and is essential for online learning. Another crucial factor is educational fairness, since poor early experiences can have an impact on students' performance and participation in the classroom. This makes remote learning a potentially useful tool for improving educational outcomes. Nevertheless, obstacles like uneven access to dependable ICT can affect how successful these programs are. Overall, remote learning can give educational systems in these regions flexibility and resilience if supportive policies and enhanced digital networks are in place. Additionally, blended learning offers potential.

4. **Healthcare:** Healthcare has benefited greatly from the evolution of connection since it has made breakthroughs possible in a number of areas:

   - **Telemedicine:** The COVID-19 epidemic has expedited the improvement of access to care, particularly for specialized consultations and in rural locations.
   - **Digital health** includes wearables for health monitoring, smartphone health apps, AI-assisted medication discovery and diagnosis, assistance for chronic illnesses, and services for the elderly.
   - **IoT in Healthcare**: By using connected devices, better patient outcomes and more efficient healthcare delivery are possible. Interoperability: It's becoming possible for patients, providers, payers, and other stakeholders to communicate seamlessly with one another.
   - **Remote Patient Monitoring:** Using connected devices, better long-term health condition management and access to preventative care are possible.

(i) Future Trends:

1. **6G Networks**: The next generation of cellular technology is called 6G, or sixth-generation wireless. In comparison to 5G networks, 6G networks will be able to use higher frequencies while offering

significantly more capacity and significantly lower latency. Supporting communications with a latency of one microsecond is one of the objectives of the 6G internet. They're anticipated to improve connectivity even more with faster speeds, reduced latency, and more sophisticated AI.

2. **Smart Environments:** Ongoing creation of IoT-connected smart cities, residences, and infrastructure. Enhancements to trash disposal, pollution prevention, energy management, smart grids, home and facility management, air and water quality, green space expansion, and emission monitoring are all part of the smart environment.

3. **Virtual and Augmented Reality (AR and VR)**: Will become more popular as a result of improved connection, which will be used for anything from remote work to gaming. In addition to improving entertainment, these immersive experiences have important uses in training, education, healthcare, and other sectors of the economy. They provide fresh approaches to data visualization, realistic scenario simulation, and remote collaboration, all of which spur innovation and advancement across a range of industries.

The constant search for quicker, better, and more effective means of communication by humans is reflected in the development of connection, which has shaped our world and spurred innovation in every field.

(j) Table Outlining the Differences Between 1G, 2G, 3G, 4G, 5G, And 6G Networks:

Feature	1G	2G	3G	4G	5G	6G
Time Period	1980s	1990s	2000s	2010s	2020s	2030s (Expected)
Technology	Analog	Digital	Digital WCDMA / CDMA2000, UMTS	Digital LTE, WiMAX	Digital NR (New Radio)	Digital Not yet defined (likely beyond NR)
Data Rate	2.4Kbps	Up to 64 Kbps	200 Kbps to 2 Mbps	100 Mbps to 1 Gbps	10 Gbps to 20 Gbps	Up to 1 Tbps
Latency	500ms	300 ms	200 ms	50 ms	1 ms	< 1 ms
Spectrum	Below 1 GHz	Below 2 GHz	1.8 to 2.5 GHz	2 to 8 GHz	24GHz to 100GHz	100GHZ to 1 THz
Modulation	Analog Modulation	TDMA, CDMA, FDMA	CDMA, FDMA	OFDMA	OFDMA, BDMA	Advanced form of OFDMA, new waveforms

Core Network	PSTN	PSTN, Packet Switching	Packet Switching (Internet)	All-IP	All-IP	Integrated AI and Quantum Communications
Main Use	Voice Calls	Voice, SMS	Mobile Internet, MMS	High-Speed Internet, Video	IoT, Enhanced Mobile Broadband	Intelligent Connectivity, Holographic Communication
Peak Throughput	2.4 Kbps	64 Kbps	2 Mbps	1 Gbps	20 Gbps	1 Tbps
Device Connectivity	Basic Mobile Phones	SMS-Capable Phones	Smartphones	Smartphones, Tablets	IoT Devices, Smart Gadgets	Intelligent Devices, Ubiquitous IoT
Bandwidth	Narrowband	Narrowband	Wideband	Broadband	Ultra-Broadband	Ultra-Broadband
Cell Capacity	Low	Low	Medium	High	Very High	Extremely High
Service Type	Analog Voice	Digital Voice, SMS	Voice, Video, Data	HD Video, Internet	4K/8K Video, IoT, AR/VR	Holographic, XR, IoE
Mobility Support	Low (Up to 80 Km/h)	Medium (Up to 200 Km/h)	Medium (Up to 350 Km/h)	High (Up to 500 Km/h)	Very High (Up to 500+ Km/h)	Ultra High (Seamless Transitions)
Source: "The Future of Connectivity: Unleashing the Power of 5G and Beyond"; GoodMan Series, (Patrick Mukosha, 2024).						

Figure 1: Table Outlining the Differences Between 1G, 2G, 3G, 4G, 5G, And 6G Networks

Note: This table summarizes the main distinctions between the generations of mobile networks, emphasizing the technological advances from 1G to the predicted 6G, including improvements in data throughput, latency, spectrum consumption, and use cases.

b. What exactly is 5G?

The fifth generation of mobile networks is called 5G. This new worldwide wireless standard follows the networks of 1G, 2G, 3G, and 4G. A new type of network, made possible by 5G, is intended to link almost everyone and everything, including machines, objects, and gadgets. The goals of 5G wireless technology are to provide more users with more consistent user experiences, ultra-low latency, vast network capacity, faster multi-Gbps peak data speeds, and increased reliability. Improved output and efficiency stimulate new user experiences and create links with new industries.

The potential maximum speed of 5G technology is 20 Gbps, compared to only 1 Gbps for 4G technology. Additionally, 5G promises reduced latency, which might enhance the functionality of various digital activities (such online gaming, videoconferencing, and self-driving cars) as well as business applications. While 4G LTE and other previous generations of cellular technology concentrated on maintaining connectivity, 5G takes connectivity a step further by offering clients connected experiences via the cloud. Cloud technologies are utilized by 5G networks, which are software-driven and virtualized. Additionally, the

5G network will make mobility easier by enabling smooth open roaming between Wi-Fi and cellular connectivity. Without user involvement, mobile users can seamlessly transition between indoor wireless networks and outdoor wireless connections.

i. 5G Network Features:

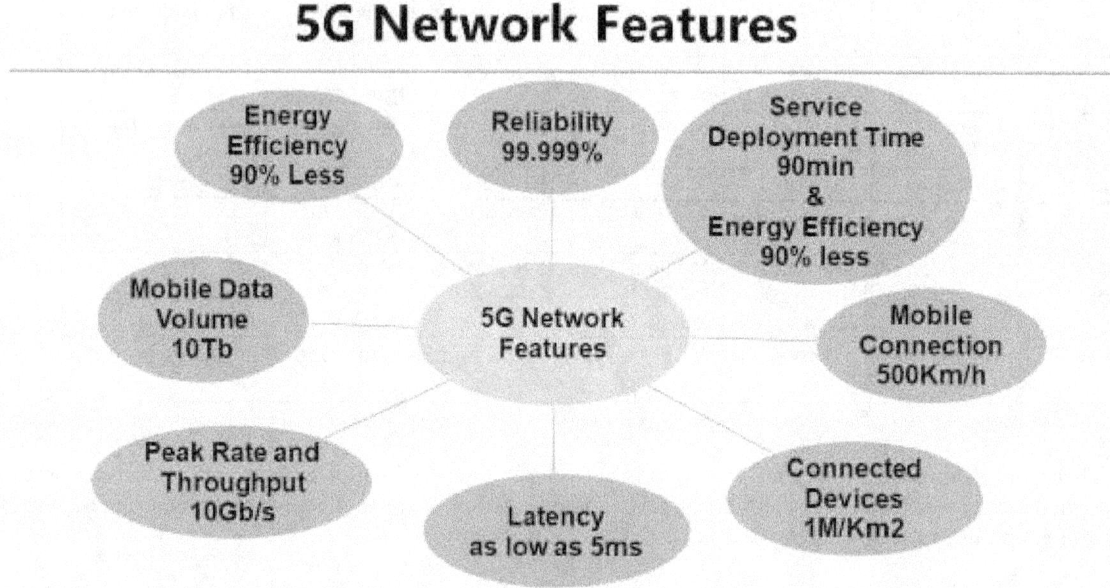

Source: "The Future of Connectivity: Unleashing the Power of 5G and Beyond", GoodMan Series, (Patrick Mukosha, 2024)

Figure 2: 5G Network Features

There are similarities between 5G and the current Wi-Fi 6 wireless standard, sometimes referred to as 802.11ax, including enhanced performance. Wi-Fi 6 radios are less expensive and offer superior geographic coverage when positioned where customers require them. These Wi-Fi 6 radios are powered by an innovative automated software-based network. In underserved rural areas and in cities where demand may exceed current 4G technology's capabilities, 5G technology should enhance connection. In order to facilitate quicker data processing, new 5G networks will also have a dense, distributed-access architecture and relocate data processing closer to the edge and the consumers.

c. How Does 5G Technology Operate?

5G technology is expected to bring about advancements in network architecture. Spectrums that were not used for 4G will be covered by 5G New Radio, the international standard for a more powerful 5G wireless air interface. Massive MIMO (multiple input, multiple output) technology, which allows multiple transmitters and receivers to carry more data at the same time, will be included into new antennas. However, the new radio frequency is not where 5G technology is restricted. It is intended to facilitate the integration of licensed and unlicensed wireless technologies in a convergent, heterogeneous network. Users will have access to more bandwidth as a result. Software-defined platforms, or 5G architectures, will control networking functions instead of hardware through software. Virtualization, cloud computing, IT, and business process automation advancements allow 5G infrastructure to be flexible and agile, enabling anytime, anywhere user access. Network slices are software-defined subnetwork constructions that can be created by 5G networks.

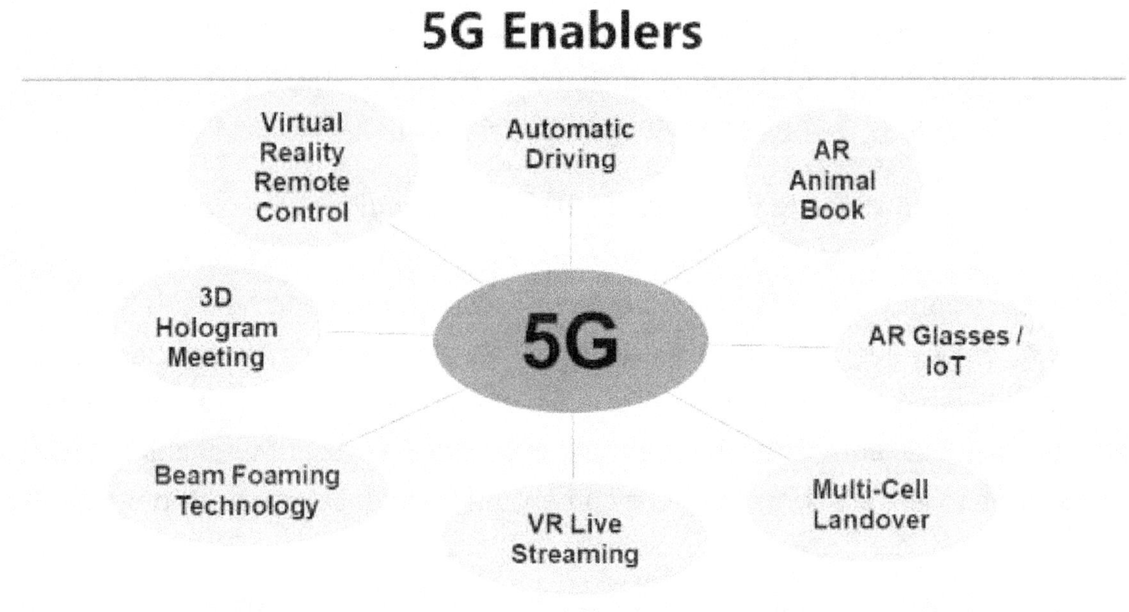

5G Enablers

Source: "The Future of Connectivity: Unleashing the Power of 5G and Beyond", GoodMan Series, (Patrick Mukosha, 2024)

Figure 3: 5G Network Enablers

Network managers can control network functionality based on users and devices by using these slices. Additionally, 5G improves digital experiences by automating tasks with machine learning (ML) capabilities. 5G networks must use automation with machine learning (ML) and, eventually, deep learning and artificial intelligence (AI) to meet the demand for response times in the order of a few nanoseconds, as seen in the case of self-driving cars. Proactive traffic and service management combined with automated provisioning will lower infrastructure costs and improve the connected user experience.

The way 5G works is as follows: *".... like all cellular networks, its service area is divided into geographic sub-areas called cells. Each cell has local antennae, which allow all wireless devices in the cell to connect to the internet and phone network via radio waves. In order to achieve its extremely high speeds, 5G uses new bands of the radio spectrum, known as "millimeter waves," which are broadcast at frequencies between 30 and 300 Gigahertz. These bands were previously only used for communication between satellites and radar systems"*. - **Patrick Mukosha**

d. Why 5G Matters

Technology is always moving in the direction of efficiency, speed, and connectedness. With each passing day, we are living in a more digitally-driven world, and the introduction of 5G networks is a significant turning point for the telecom industry. Its impact is revolutionary, offering unmatched connectivity and an infrastructure that has the potential to completely change economies, lifestyles, and industries.

IT professionals can attest that *5G technology is a significant development in mobile networks. Its significance goes beyond only enabling speedier internet.* In order to fully appreciate the significance of 5G technology, we must comprehend how this generational leap differs from earlier ones. 5G is expected to surpass earlier network generations in speed. Still, 5G has benefits beyond speed. Low latency is another feature of 5G that enables connections and data sharing very instantly between 5G-enabled apps and communications. Here are some strong arguments in favor of 5G, supported by real-world examples:

    i. **Ultra-Fast Speed and Large Bandwidth:**
- **Example:**
  - **High-Definition Downloads and Streaming:** Users may stream 4K video without buffering and download full HD movies in a matter of seconds thanks to speeds that could reach up to 10 Gbps. Large files and high-quality video content are frequent in professional and entertainment settings, and this improvement changes the way users interact with these settings.

    ii. **Low Latency**:
- **Example:**

- o **AR/VR with Online Gaming:** Milliseconds might mean the difference between winning and losing in competitive online gaming. The real-time responsiveness provided by 5G's low latency (~1 millisecond) is essential for applications like *Virtual Reality* (VR) and *Augmented Reality* (AR) games. Applications for AR and VR, such as training simulations and real-time navigation, depend on this responsiveness to be immersive.

iii. **Deep Device Networking:**

- **Example:**
  - o **Internet of Things and Smart Cities:** *Up to a million devices may be supported by 5G per square kilometer,* which will help smart cities expand. These include smart meters that track and regulate energy use, networked traffic signals that lessen traffic, and Internet of Things (IoT) sensors that enhance waste management effectiveness and public safety.

iv. **Enhanced Mobile Broadband:**

- **Example:**
  - o **Teleconferencing and Remote Work:** The COVID-19 pandemic made it clear how crucial dependable remote work capabilities are. *5G supports a more productive and connected distant workforce by enabling continuous video conferencing and collaborative tools without the lags and disturbances associated with 4G.*

v. **Network Slicing:**

- **Example:**
  - o **Specific Networks for Emergencies**: Network slicing makes it possible to design virtual networks that are suited to certain requirements. For example, emergency services can have a dedicated slice with ultra-low latency and guaranteed bandwidth, which guarantees dependable communication during emergencies free from interference from other traffic.

vi. **Industrial Automation and IoT:**

- **Example:**
  - o **Manufacturing and Smart Factories:** 5G makes it possible for sophisticated IoT applications in the manufacturing sector, like predictive maintenance, which lowers costs and downtime by using

sensors on machines to identify problems before they become major ones. 5G enables real-time automation and monitoring in smart factories, improving both output and security.

vii. **Improved Healthcare Services:**
- **Example:**
  - **Telemedicine and Remote Surgery:** High-quality video consultations are a key component of telemedicine services and are essential for precise diagnosis and treatment. Surgeons can use remote surgery to control robotic tools in real-time from a distance, which could save lives in places without access to specialized medical care.

viii. **Autonomous Vehicles:**
- **Example:**
  - **Vehicle-to-Everything (V2X) Communication:** 5G enables V2X communication, which is a means of improving efficiency and safety through vehicle-to-vehicle and road infrastructure connection. Autonomous driving depends on this real-time data interchange, which also helps to improve traffic flow and reduce accidents.

ix. **Energy Efficiency and Sustainability:**
- **Example:**
  - **Smart Grid Management:** As an illustration, consider 5G's potential to increase power grid efficiency through smart grid management, which uses real-time data from several sources to optimize energy distribution and cut waste. This makes energy use more economical and sustainable.

x. **Innovation and Economic Growth:**
- **Example:**
  - **Startups and New Business:** Models 5G's capabilities have the potential to drive innovation in a number of industries, resulting in the formation of new businesses and business models. For example, new uses in telemedicine, smart agriculture, and AR-based tourism may surface and spur economic expansion and employment development.

xi. **The 5G Enabler:**

5G Enablers

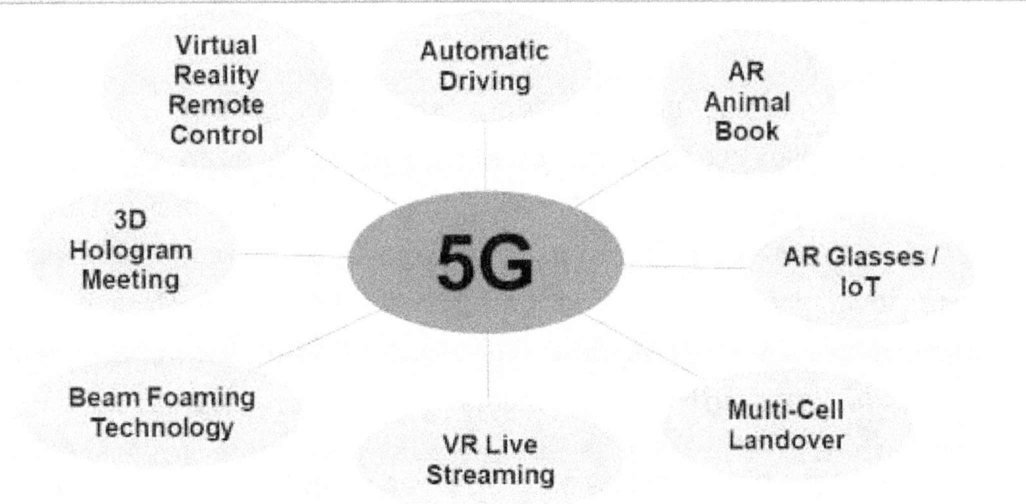

Source: "The Future of Connectivity: Unleashing the Power of 5G and Beyond", GoodMan Series, (Patrick Mukosha, 2024)

Figure 4: The 5G Enabler

In summary, the reason *5G is important is because it offers the infrastructure required for the upcoming wave of technological advancements*. It makes solutions faster, more dependable, and more integrated, which can revolutionize a number of facets of daily life and business operations. 5G will have a significant and wide-ranging impact on everything from smart city development and healthcare to entertainment and distant work. In addition to meeting present needs, this technology paves the way for yet-to-be-imagined future developments.

Chapter 1: Understanding 5G Technology

1.1. The Basics of 5G

5G, or fifth generation cellular networks, *is a wireless standard used worldwide*. All cellular networks use radio waves to transmit encoded data. Radio waves are separated into bands and have various frequencies. While 4G and other previous generations relied on low- and mid-band frequencies for operation, 5G is capable of operating on millimeter wave (also known as low-, mid-, and high-band) frequencies. *While higher frequencies are much faster yet have a much smaller range and find it difficult to pass through objects, lower frequencies are able to go farther and permeate past obstacles at relatively low speeds.*

Although *5G allows for the utilization of large areas of high-frequency spectrum that are currently unoccupied, it also includes new technologies and methods for merging existing spectrum segments.* At its most basic, 5G seems and feels a lot like 4G. Fifth-generation wireless technology, or 5G, is the most recent development in mobile networks. Compared to 4G and 3G, it is intended to greatly improve the speed, coverage, and responsiveness of wireless networks.

Below is a summary of the main features of 5G:

1.1.1. **Speed:**

It is anticipated that 5G networks would surpass 4G in speed, with potential *peak speeds reaching up to 20 Gbps*. With this high-speed capacity, downloads and uploads may be completed more quickly, facilitating smooth streaming of HD videos, real-time gaming, and the speedy transfer of big data files.

1.1.2. **Latency:**

In 5G networks, latency—*the amount of time it takes for data to move from one place to another*—is drastically decreased. While 4G had an average delay of about 50 milliseconds, 5G promises to attain latencies as low as 1 millisecond. Applications that need real-time feedback, such augmented reality (AR) experiences, remote surgery, and driverless cars, depend on this almost instantaneous response time.

1.1.3. **Capacity:**

5G networks are *built to support a huge number of devices at once*. This capacity expansion helps the Internet of Things (IoT) ecosystem, which is predicted to grow to billions of connected devices, ranging from industrial sensors to smart home appliances.

1.1.4. **Spectrum:**

A *wider range of frequencies*, including low-, mid-, and high-band (millimeter wave) spectrums, are used by Spectrum 5G:

- **Low-Band:** Wide coverage is provided by low-band spectrum, which works well in suburban and rural locations.
- **Mid-Band:** spectrum is appropriate for urban settings because it strikes a compromise between coverage and speed.
- **High-Band:** Although it has limited coverage and penetration, high-band (millimeter wave) spectrum is perfect for some high-demand applications and densely inhabited locations because it offers incredibly high speeds and low latency.

1.1.5. **Network Slicing:**

Network slicing, which *enables the development of many virtual networks inside a single physical 5G network*, is supported by 5G. Every slice can be tailored to match the unique needs of various services or apps, guaranteeing effective resource management and peak performance.

1.1.6. **Efficiency in Energy Use:**

Energy-saving technologies built into *5G technology aim to lower power usage in connected devices as well as network infrastructure*. Advanced power management algorithms and more effective transmission methods enable this.

1.1.7. **Improved Connectivity:**

Consistent and dependable connectivity is what 5G promises to deliver, even in difficult situations like packed stadiums, busy cities, and fast-moving transportation (like cars and trains). Modern technologies like large MIMO (Multiple Input Multiple Output) and beamforming enable this enhanced connectivity.

1.1.8. **Applications:**

Many applications and services that were not possible with earlier generations are now possible thanks to the improvements provided by 5G, including:

- **Smart Cities:** Better public services, smart lighting, and more effective traffic control thanks to increased connectivity.
- **Healthcare:** Robotic surgery, telemedicine, and remote patient monitoring.
- **Automotive:** V2X (vehicle-to-everything) connectivity, automated driving, and connected autos.
- **Industry 4.0:** Includes automated logistics, intelligent manufacturing, and real-time process monitoring.

In summary, wireless communication technology has advanced significantly with 5G, which promises lower latency, quicker speeds, and support for a large number of devices. These advancements will open the door for cutting-edge services and applications that will revolutionize a number of industries and improve digital life in general.

1.2. How 5G Differs from Previous Generations

In a number of important areas, 5G technology differs significantly from 4G, 3G, and 2G mobile network generations. Governments, IT companies, and stakeholders from a variety of industries are eager to jump on the 5G bandwagon, as its benefits far exceed its negatives. Applications and innovations that greatly accelerate economic growth and technical progress can be enabled by a fully operational 5G network. Compared to earlier generations, there is much more at risk with the switch to 5G. This is because, in contrast to the successive generations that came before it, 5G diverges from the present generation in a more noticeable way. But *the shift to 5G will be a long and difficult process that will take years and billions of dollars in capital expenditures.*

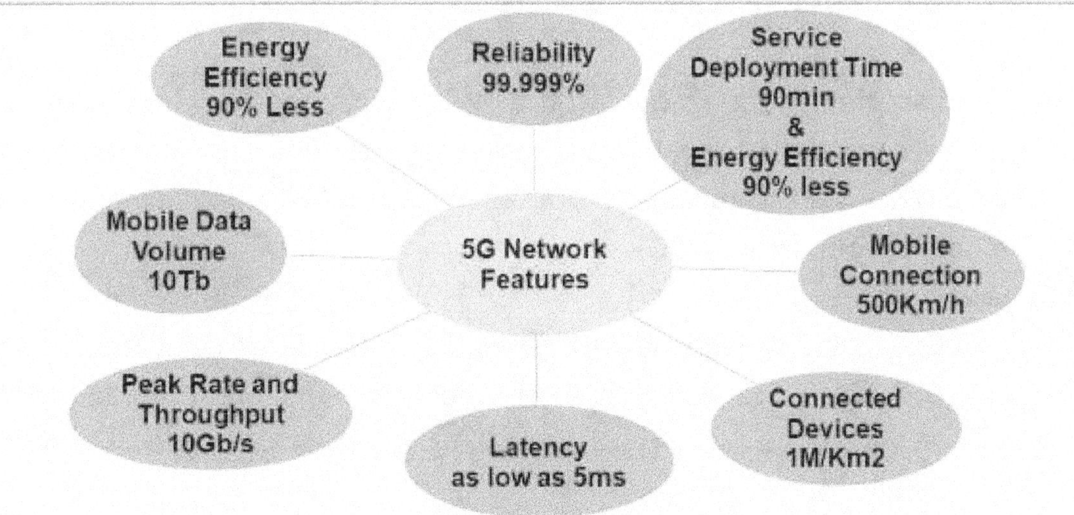

Figure 5: 5G Network Features

Here is a thorough comparison that shows the variations and includes striking examples:

1.2.1. **Speed:**

- **2G (GSM):** Voice communication was the main focus of 2G (GSM), which also brought basic data capabilities with up to 50 Kbps of speed.
- **3G (UMTS):** Faster data rates of up to 2 Mbps allow for video calling and mobile internet access.
- **4G (LTE):** With peak internet speeds of up to 1 Gbps, 4G (LTE) has made it possible to stream HD videos and browse the web more quickly.
- **5G:** Provides previously unheard-of speeds of up to 20 Gbps, allowing for flawless VR/AR experiences and the rapid download of high definition movies in a matter of seconds.
- **Example:** Downloading a nearly two-gigabyte HD movie:
  - **4G:** About two to three minutes.
  - **5G:** A brief moment.

1.2.2. **Latency:**

- **2G/3G:** Latencies between 300 and 100 milliseconds render real-time applications unfeasible.

- **4G:** Improved video conversations and online gaming by lowering latency to about 50 milliseconds.
- **5G:** Purposes to achieve 1 milliseconds latencies, which are critical for real-time applications.
- **Example:** Motion sickness in a virtual reality game where there is a 50 millisecond (4G) lag between the user's actions and the reaction. Such problems are eliminated by the seamless and real-time experience with 1 millisecond latency (5G).

1.2.3. Capacity:

- **2G:** Capable of handling only basic SMS and voice calls, but limited capacity.
- **3G:** Enhanced capability to enable mobile internet and early smartphones.
- **4G:** Even more capacity, allowing for the use of several devices and large amounts of data.
- **5G:** Designed to serve the vast IoT ecosystem by handling an enormous number of linked devices.
- **Example:** 5G can enable millions of networked devices in a smart city, including sensors, cameras, and smart meters. These devices can communicate in real-time to manage energy consumption, improve traffic flow, and monitor air quality.

1.2.4. Spectrum Utilisation:

- **2G:** Narrowband frequencies, mostly in the 900 MHz range.
- **3G:** Greater usage of the 1.8 GHz and 2.1 GHz bands, among other spectrum.
- **4G:** Makes use of a wider spectrum, which includes bands as high as 2.6 GHz.
- **5G:** Makes use of millimeter wave, or 24–100 GHz, high-band (24–100 GHz), and mid-band (1-6 GHz).
- **Example:** Although it has a restricted range, high-band (millimeter wave) spectrum in densely populated areas offers very fast data speeds and low latency. Because of this, it's perfect for uses like stadiums or concert halls where a lot of people need high-speed connectivity at once.

1.2.5. Network Architecture:

- **2G/3G:** The conventional, centralized network architecture of 2G and 3G.
- **4G:** LTE Advanced introduces a degree of decentralization.

- **5G:** An architecture that is fully integrated, versatile, and capable of network slicing.
- **Example:** 5G network slicing enables the creation of specialized virtual networks for certain uses. For example, one slice can be designed for high reliability and ultra-low latency for autonomous vehicles, while another slice can prioritize high bandwidth for video streaming.

1.2.6. **Enhanced Mobile Broadband (eMBB):**

- **2G, 3G, and 4G:** Gradual advancements in mobile broadband.
- **5G:** Virtual reality (VR), augmented reality (AR), and 4K/8K video streaming are all supported by 5G, a significant improvement.
- **Example:** High bandwidth and low latency are needed to watch a live 8K sports event in virtual reality. The eMBB capabilities of 5G offer the performance required to smoothly transmit such high-resolution material.

1.2.7. **Ultra-Reliable Low-Latency Communication (URLLC):**

- **2G, 3G, and 4G:** Low-latency, high-reliability applications are not well supported by 2G, 3G, or 4G networks.
- **5G:** Especially made to accommodate URLLC for applications that are vital to mission success.
- **Example:** A physician conducting remote surgery can use robotic instruments that are managed via a 5G network. Remote surgery is safe and possible because of the surgical instruments' ultra-low latency and great dependability, which guarantee that they react to the doctor's motions instantly.

In summary, in terms of speed, latency, capacity, spectrum usage, network architecture, and particular use cases like improved mobile broadband and incredibly dependable low-latency communication, 5G performs noticeably better than prior generations. These developments open up previously unthinkable new services and applications, revolutionizing a number of industries and improving people's digital experiences all across the world.

1.3 The 5G Spectrum

Communication service providers *(CSPs) must employ a variety of multiple frequency bands to deliver 5G services, as connectivity is reshaping our environment.* For CSPs, 5G brings with it some new challenges. On the one hand, 5G networks enable lower latency and higher mobile broadband rates, opening the door for new applications like the Internet of Things (IoT), artificial intelligence (AI), and the Metaverse. However, for these new services to become a reality, 5G will need CSPs to have access to large amounts of spectrum.

The *Global System for Mobile Communications Association* (GSMA), a global trade association that represents the global mobile communications sector, reports that as of the beginning of 2023, 515 operators were investing in 5G globally, with 243 commercial 5G launches. The GSMA advises governments and regulatory bodies in charge of allocating 5G spectrum to allocate 80–100 MHz of contiguous spectrum per operator in prime 5G bands and roughly 1 GHz of millimeter wave spectrum per operator.

Compared to earlier generations of mobile networks, *5G operates across a larger frequency band, enabling it to provide a combination of faster speeds, more capacity, and lower latency.* Three primary bands comprise the 5G spectrum: *Low-Band, Mid-Band, and High-Band* (millimeter wave). Every band has its own unique qualities and best applications.

1.3.1. Low-Band Spectrum

    a. **Frequency Range:** 600 MHz, 700 MHz, and 800 MHz, on average, below 1 GHz.

    b. **Features:**

- **Wide Coverage:** Low-band frequencies are perfect for offering wide coverage in rural and suburban areas since they can travel great distances and successfully penetrate structures.
- **Reduced Speeds:** Compared to mid-band and high-band frequencies, they have lower data speeds even though they have good coverage.

    c. **Use Cases:**

- **Rural Connectivity**: provides dependable internet connection and mobile service in outlying places.
- **Indoor Coverage**: Better indoor signal strength is provided by the interior coverage, which penetrates walls and other obstructions.
- **Example:** in rural areas, low-band spectrum can offer crucial connection for both private and commercial purposes, guaranteeing that even the most isolated areas have access to the internet and mobile services.

1.3.2. Mid-Band Spectrum

    a. **Frequency Range:** around 2.5 GHz, 3.5 GHz, and 3.7-4.2 GHz (usually around these three frequencies).

b. **Features:**
- **Balanced Speed and Coverage:** Provides a strong mix between capacity, speed, and coverage, making it appropriate for both urban and suburban settings.
- **Moderate Penetration:** Not as good as low-band frequencies, but still able to penetrate buildings more effectively than high-band frequencies.

c. **Use Cases:**
- **Urban Connectivity:** Improved mobile broadband services are made available in cities and suburban regions through urban connectivity.
- **Enterprise Applications:** Provides support for corporate applications that need a relatively fast and dependable connection.
- **Example:** Mid-band spectrum can manage heavy traffic volumes in a busy city, guaranteeing consumers quick and dependable internet access for online activities such as streaming and video calls.

1.3.3. High-Band Spectrum (Millimeter Wave):

a. **Frequency range:** 24 GHz to 100 GHz is the frequency range (usually about 26 GHz, 28 GHz, and 39 GHz)

b. **Features:**
- **High Speeds:** Able to transmit incredibly high data rates, this makes it appropriate for applications that need dependable and quick connections.
- **Restricted Range:** Has a reduced range and is less able to pass through foliage and buildings.
- **High Capacity:** Suitable for densely populated locations, it can support a large number of devices in a compact area.

c. **Use Cases:**
- **Dense Urban Areas:** Offers fast internet access In congested locations including city centers, stadiums, and airports.
- **Fixed Wireless Access:** Provides high-speed internet wirelessly, providing a substitute for fiber-optic broadband in households and businesses.
- **Example:** High band spectrum can guarantee that thousands of fans at a big sports stadium can concurrently watch live video, post updates on social media, and access other web services without any lag.

1.3.4. Spectrum Allocation and Utilization:

1. **Dynamic Spectrum Sharing (DSS):** 5G networks can share spectrum with 4G LTE networks that are currently in place by using DSS. By *using the same frequency channels, this enables carriers to smoothly switch from 4G to 5G, maximizing the utilization of available spectrum resources without interfering with currently offered services.*

2. **Carrier Aggregation:** A 5G method called carrier aggregation *combines many frequency bands to increase bandwidth and boost transmission throughput.* By doing this, networks are able to take advantage of several spectrum bands at the same time, improving coverage and performance.

In summary, 5G covers a wide range of frequencies, including low-, mid-, and high-band frequencies, each with specific benefits and uses. 5G's diverse approach makes it possible to provide huge machine-type communication, ultra-reliable low-latency communication, and improved mobile broadband, supporting a wide range of use cases and revolutionizing how we connect and engage with the digital world.

Chapter 2: The 5G Infrastructure

Technology is always moving in the direction of *efficiency, speed, and connectedness*. With each passing day, we are living in a more digitally-driven world, and the introduction of 5G networks is a significant turning point for the telecom industry. Its impact is revolutionary, offering unmatched connectivity and an infrastructure that has the potential to completely change economies, lifestyles, and industries.

The process of constructing a 5G network is intricate and involves several steps, each needing a particular set of technologies, knowledge, and equipment. Here is a thorough explanation of the essential elements and procedures needed to construct a 5G network, along with real-world examples:

2.1.1. Spectrum Allocation:

- **Description:** *The radio frequencies used for communication are referred to as the spectrum.* Millimeter waves, or high-frequency bands over 24 GHz, mid-frequency bands between 1 and 6 GHz, and low-frequency bands below 1 GHz are used for 5G. 5G, in contrast to its predecessors, uses higher frequency bands—such as millimeter waves (mmWave)—to provide quicker data transfer. These waves provide enormous bandwidth for applications that require a lot of data by operating in the 24GHz to 100GHz range. Governments and regulatory agencies provide frequencies to telecom companies in order to ensure effective use and little interference, which makes spectrum distribution crucial.
- **Example:** The Federal Communications Commission (FCC) in the United States auctions spectrum to telecommunications businesses. For example, Verizon may buy certain high-frequency spectrum to guarantee lower latency and quicker data throughput.

2.1.2. Infrastructure Deployment:

2.1.2.1. Base Stations and Small Cells:

- **Description:** To enable high-speed 5G services in metropolitan areas, small cells are added to traditional cell towers. Low-power cellular radio access nodes that cover tiny areas are known as *Small Cells*.

- **Example:** To improve network capacity and offer dense coverage, small cell installations may be seen on buildings, streetlights, and other structures in a city like New York.

2.1.2.2. Massive MIMO:

- **Description:** Using multiple antennas, *Multiple-Input Multiple-Output* (MIMO) technology allows for the simultaneous transmission and reception of more data.
- **Example:** Thousands of people can stream video simultaneously without service degradation at a single 5G base station in a packed stadium thanks to massive MIMO technology.

2.1.3. Fiber Optic Backhaul:

- **Description:** To ensure high-speed data transfer, base stations must be connected to the core network via fiber optic cables.
- **Example:** Consider installing fiber optic cables beneath city streets or across rural areas to link newly installed 5G macro towers and small cells to the main network.

2.1.4. Edge Computing:

- **Description:** By *decreasing the distance data travels, edge computing, a paradigm where data processing happens closer to the end-user, minimizes latency.* This idea is further developed by *network slicing,* which divides a single physical network into several virtual networks. Every segment meets various application needs, guaranteeing top-notch functionality for various services, ranging from industrial automation to augmented reality.
- **Example:** Consider setting up edge servers at neighborhood data centers in urban areas to manage data processing for augmented reality and driverless car applications, guaranteeing quick reaction times.

2.1.5. Upgrades to the Core Network:

- **Description:** The new 5G features, including network slicing, require an upgrade to the core network, which controls connections and data routing.
- **Example:** consider putting in place a virtualized, software-defined core network that can assign resources dynamically and build virtual

networks customized for particular uses, such as streaming high-definition video or the Internet of Things.

2.1.6. Techniques for Deployment:

1. Non-Standalone (NSA) 5G:

- **Overview:** NSA deploys 5G services more quickly and affordably by utilizing the current 4G LTE infrastructure.
- **Example:** a telecom company such as AT&T may first deploy NSA 5G in large cities to take advantage of the current 4G towers and then progressively deploy standalone 5G infrastructure.

2. Standalone (SA) 5G:

- **Overview:** Full 5G functionality is provided via SA 5G, which functions independently of the current 4G infrastructure.
- **Example:** Consider constructing new 5G networks in greenfield areas—new constructions devoid of any existing infrastructure—in order to provide all of the advantages of 5G right now.

2.1.7. Testing and Optimisation

- **Overview:** To make sure the network satisfies user expectations and performance standards; extensive testing is carried out. Optimizing the network entails adjusting its capacity, coverage, and efficiency.
- **Example:** network engineers can monitor signal strength, data rates, and latency using software tools and drive testing (driving around with testing equipment) and make necessary improvements.

2.1.8. Regulatory Compliance and Security:

- **Overview:** Guaranteeing that the network conforms to regional laws and is safe from online attacks.
- **Example:** putting strong authentication procedures in place, network slicing to separate traffic, and encryption in place to safeguard user information and network integrity.

2.1.9. Consumer and Enterprise Services

- **Overview:** Providing businesses and consumers with 5G services, such as huge IoT connection, ultra reliable low latency communications, and improved mobile broadband.
- **Examples** include 5G home internet services offered by telecom companies like T-Mobile and the use of private 5G networks for real-time automation and monitoring in sectors like manufacturing.

2.1.10. **Continuous Improvement:**

- **Overview:** The network undergoes periodic updates and upgrades to include novel technology and broaden its reach.
- **Example:** Introducing new features like network slicing for certain enterprise applications, extending coverage to rural areas, or deploying updates over the air (OTA) to base stations and devices to improve performance.

In summary, the construction of a 5G network is a complex process that includes advanced technology deployment, regulatory navigating, ongoing optimization, and strategic planning. As a result, a network with previously unheard-of data rates, minimal latency, and a large number of linked devices is created, opening the door to creative services and applications in a variety of industries.

2.2. Small Cells and Massive MIMO

The flood of applications that require massive amounts of data has made it difficult for next-generation cellular systems to maintain high data rates while using less energy and maintaining strong service quality. Small cells and massive MIMO are the most advanced methods to deal with these issues. By installing a huge number of antennas at the base station, wireless networks can achieve greater spectral and energy efficiency. This technology is known as *Massive MIMO*. On the other hand, *Small Cells* shorten the distance between the user and the base station, enabling fast data rates and good coverage at lower transmit power consumption. Here is an in-depth explanation of the two technologies.

2.2.1. Small Cells:

- **Definition:** Small cells are low-power cellular radio access nodes that typically have a range of a few hundred meters to several hundred meters. They can operate in both licensed and unlicensed Spectrum. They are crucial for increasing network coverage and capacity, especially in crowded cities where conventional macro cell towers are unable to meet demand.

2.2.2. Small Cell Types

1. **Femtocells:** The smallest variety, with a coverage of up to 10 meters, are intended for use in homes or small businesses.

2. **Picocells:** A little bigger, 200-meter-wide coverage that works well in offices and compact spaces.

3. **Microcells:** More expansive than Picocells, they can cover up to two kilometers and are utilized in public areas like parks and malls.

   - **Examples:**
     - **Urban Deployment:** To provide high-speed 5G coverage in places where it is prohibitive or impossible to put large cell towers, tiny cells are mounted on streetlights, utility poles, and building walls in cities like New York.
     - **Indoor Coverage:** To provide robust and reliable network coverage indoors, where signals from macro towers could be difficult to penetrate, shopping centers, airports, and stadiums install tiny cells.
     - **Enhancements for Rural places:** To extend coverage and improve service in places where large cell towers are not cost-effective, tiny cells can be installed atop existing structures like barns or silos.

2.2.3. Massive MIMO (Multiple Input Multiple Output)

2.2.3.1. Description: A huge number of antennas at the base station are used in massive MIMO, a sophisticated antenna technique, to send and receive more data simultaneously. This is a crucial part of 5G technology since it greatly boosts the network's capacity and efficiency.

2.2.3.2. How It Operates

- **Conventional MIMO:** Increases signal strength and dependability by transmitting and receiving data using a small number of antennas (2x2, 4x4).
- **Massive MIMO:** This technology significantly improves network capacity and performance by transmitting and receiving numerous data streams concurrently using dozens or even hundreds of antennas (64x64, 128x128).

2.2.3.3. Example:

- **Dense Urban Areas:** Massive MIMO technology allows a single base station to serve thousands of users streaming video, conducting video calls, and utilizing data-intensive applications without sacrificing service quality in crowded areas like Times Square.

- o **Big Venues:** Tens of thousands of people may enjoy strong connectivity at sports stadiums and music halls thanks to huge MIMO, which also makes it possible for everyone to exchange real-time updates, images, and videos.
- o **Smart Factories:** By linking hundreds of sensors and equipment, massive MIMO offers real-time monitoring and automation in industrial settings. This enables effective and continuous data communication for industrial Internet of things applications.

2.2.3. Principal Advantages

2.2.3.1. Small Cells:

a. **Enhanced Coverage:** Increases network coverage in regions where there aren't enough macro cells.

b. **Enhanced Capacity**: Increases network capacity by transferring traffic from macro cells.

c. **Minimal Latency:** Lowers latency by minimizing the distance that data must travel.

2.2.3.2. Large-scale MIMO:

a. **Greater Capacity:** Allows for the support of more users and devices at once.

b. **Increased Efficiency:** Increases spectral efficiency, enabling the transmission of more data with the same amount of bandwidth.

c. **Improved Reliability:** Beamforming, which focuses signals on certain users rather than broadcasting in all directions, strengthens signals and lowers interference.

2.2.4. Real-World Deployment:

2.2.4.1. Case Study: Verizon's 5G Rollout:

- **Small Cells:** To support its 5G network, Verizon has started installing thousands of tiny cells in major American cities including Chicago and Los Angeles. To achieve intensive coverage, these tiny cells are frequently installed on building facades and utility poles.
- **Massive MIMO:** Verizon uses Massive MIMO antennas in its 5G network to improve capacity and performance, especially in busy places like commercial districts and sports arenas. The network can support many

simultaneous connections and provide high-speed data services thanks to these antennas.

2.2.4.2. Case Study: 5G Network in South Korea

- **Small Cells:** One of the pioneers in the rollout of 5G, South Korea, has made considerable use of tiny cells to provide complete 5G coverage in places such as Seoul. To enable continuous communication, small cells are placed in shopping centers, residential areas, and subways.
- **Massive MIMO:** To improve network performance and enable applications like Augmented Reality (AR) and Virtual Reality (VR), which need high data rates and low latency, Korean telecom carriers like SK Telecom deploy massive MIMO technology.

In summary, *massive MIMO and small cells are essential to 5G networks' success*. In densely populated locations, massive MIMO greatly improves the network's efficiency and capability to handle numerous connections at once, while small cells provide extensive coverage and enhanced capacity. When combined, they provide the dependable, fast, and low-latency connectivity that 5G promises.

2.3. Edge Computing and its Role in 5G

Definition: The term "*Edge Computing*" describes the approach of processing data less dependently on centralized data centers, and instead closer to the source or "edge" of the network. Edge computing improves reliability, performance, and latency by relocating processing and storage closer to the point of data generation.

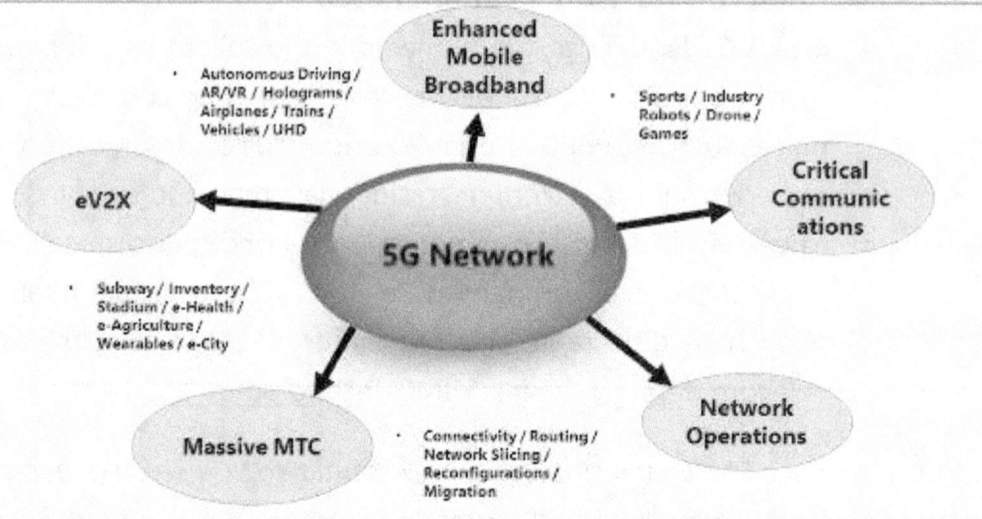

Source: "The Future of Connectivity: Unleashing the Power of 5G and Beyond", GoodMan Series, (Patrick Mukosha, 2024).

Figure 6: 5G Network - Mission Critical Applications

2.3.1. The Function of Edge Computing in 5G:

2.3.1.1. Lower Latency:

- **Description:** The capacity of edge computing to significantly lower latency is one of its main benefits. *Edge computing reduces the amount of time that data must travel back and forth between the device and the server by processing data close to the source.*

- **Example:** edge computing in autonomous cars can handle sensor and video data locally on the car or at neighboring edge servers. This makes it possible for real-time decision-making, which is necessary to guarantee passenger safety and includes tasks like obstacle detection and safe navigation.

2.3.1.2. Increased Reliability and Speed

- **Description:** Edge computing relieves network congestion and offloads traffic from central servers to enable high-speed data processing and transfer.

  Example: a smart city's surveillance cameras produce a lot of video data. Edge servers have the capability to process video locally in order to identify faces or detect anomalies, thereby minimizing the load on the core network and guaranteeing prompt reactions to security issues. This eliminates the need to send all footage to a remote data center.

2.3.1.3. **Enhanced Efficiency of Bandwidth**:

- **Description:** Edge computing minimizes the amount of data that needs to be transmitted over the network by processing data locally, freeing up bandwidth for other applications.
- **Example:** Edge computing enables local data processing in industrial IoT applications, such a factory with multiple sensors monitoring equipment performance. By sending only pertinent data to the cloud—such as warnings or summary reports—bandwidth is used more efficiently and urgent information is delivered on time.

2.3.1.4. **Assistance with Complex Applications:**

- **Description:** Edge computing *makes it possible for cutting-edge applications like Virtual Reality (VR), Augmented Reality (AR), and Gaming that demand low latency and real-time processing.*
- **Example:** edge servers can process AR data locally to give personnel real-time overlays and instructions when doing AR-based maintenance on industrial machines. Because of the minimal latency, which guarantees that the AR overlays are sensitive and move in unison with the technician's motions, this enables precise and efficient repairs.

2.3.2. **Examples of Edge Computing in 5G Real World:**

2.3.2.1. **Autonomous Vehicles**:

- **Scenario:** In order to handle data from LIDAR, cameras, and radar sensors in real-time, a self-driving automobile uses edge computing. This data is analyzed by edge servers in the car or adjacent roadside equipment to make split-second decisions like braking for a pedestrian or maneuvering through traffic.
- **Benefit:** By lowering latency, this localized data processing improves the dependability and safety of autonomous driving systems.

2.3.2.2. **Smart Cities:**

- **Scenario:** Real-time traffic pattern analysis and optimal traffic flow optimization are possible with smart traffic lights that have edge computing capabilities. Furthermore, edge servers have the capability to handle information from air quality sensors in order to promptly notify locals about pollution.

- **Benefit:** By enhancing public health and transportation efficiency without overtaxing the central network, these applications improve urban living.

2.3.2.3. **Healthcare:**

- **Scenario:** Wearable technology is used in telemedicine to monitor patients' vital signs and analyze the data locally using edge computing. When the system notices an abnormality, like an irregular heartbeat, it can notify medical professionals right away and initiate an emergency response.
- **Benefit:** This real-time data analysis eliminates the need for continuous data transfer to central servers and guarantees timely medical action, which might be crucial for patient outcomes.

2.3.2.4. **Industrial Automation:**

- **Scenario:** Edge computing is used in a manufacturing plant to monitor production lines and machinery. Edge servers analyze sensor data to identify problems with the equipment or anticipate maintenance requirements, enabling quick response.
- **Benefit:** By lowering maintenance expenses and downtime, this guarantees effective and continuous operations.

2.3.3. **Integrating with 5G:**

2.3.3.1. **Network Slicing:**

- **Description:** *5G enables the establishment of several virtual networks, each suited for a particular set of applications or services, on a single physical infrastructure.*
- **Example:** An edge computing application for emergency services can be isolated from other network traffic, such as consumer video streaming, and have its own dedicated network slice with assured low latency and high reliability.

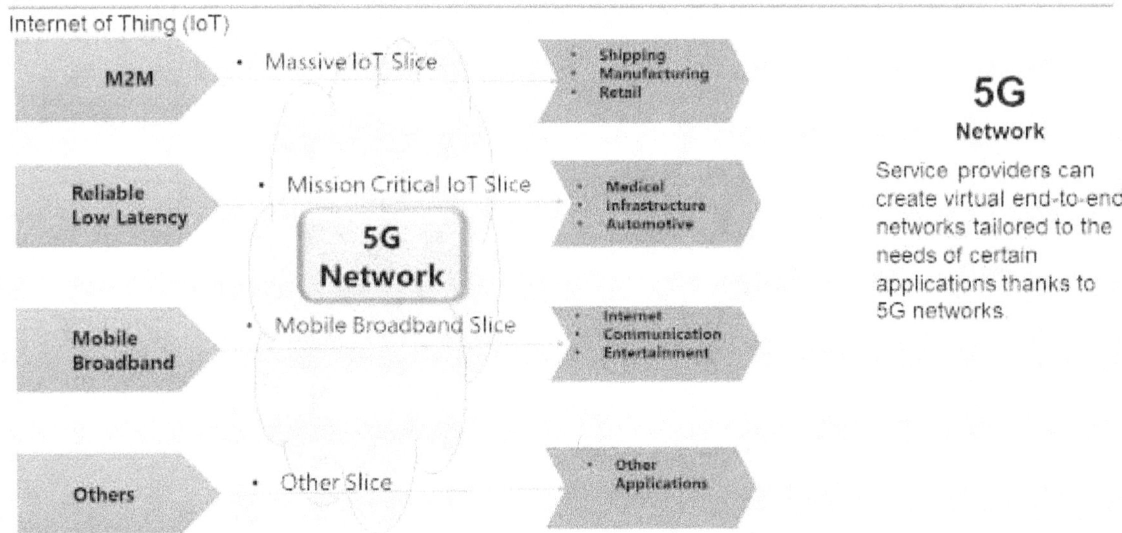

Source: "The Future of Connectivity: Unleashing the Power of 5G and Beyond", GoodMan Series, (Patrick Mukosha, 2024)

Figure 7: 5G Network Slicing

2.3.3.2. Ultra-Reliable Low-Latency Communication (URLLC):

- **Description:** The support for URLLC, which is necessary for applications needing real-time data processing and low latency, is built into 5G networks.
- **Example:** Precise control over robotic arms and other machinery in a factory is made possible by URLLC-enabled edge computing, which guarantees secure and effective manufacturing procedures.

2.3.3.3. Massive Machine-Type Communication (mMTC)

- **Description:** 5G's mMTC feature allows it to link a large number of devices at once.
- **Example:** thousands of sensors track temperature, crop health, and soil moisture in a smart agricultural setup. By processing this data locally, edge computing maximizes crop productivity and resource efficiency by automating irrigation systems and giving farmers useful information.

In summary, the 5G ecosystem's edge computing is essential for a variety of applications that demand fast speeds, minimal latency, and economical bandwidth use. Edge computing improves the speed and capabilities of 5G networks by processing data closer to the source, enabling cutting-edge technology and enhancing user experiences in a variety of industries.

Chapter 3: Applications of 5G in Various Industries

3.1. 5G in Healthcare

5G technology is transforming healthcare by allowing multiple devices to be connected at once, lowering latency, and speeding up data flow. These are a few striking instances that highlight how 5G will affect healthcare:

3.1.1. **Remote Surgery:**

3.1.1.1. **Telesurgery as an Example:**

- **Scenario:** A patient in a remote Montana hospital undergoes a complicated surgical procedure performed by a board-certified surgeon in New York.
- **How 5G Is Beneficial:** Real-time communication between the surgeon and robotic surgical equipment is ensured by 5G's ultra-low latency. This makes precise control and fast feedback possible, both of which are essential for sensitive procedures. A clear and comprehensive image of the operating area is available to the surgeon thanks to high-definition video streaming made possible by the high bandwidth.

3.1.2. **Telemedicine:**

3.1.2.1. **Example: Virtual Consultations:**

- **Scenario:** A specialist in a city provides a video consultation with a patient in a remote town.
- **How 5G Is Beneficial:** 5G's fast internet guarantees lag-free, crystal-clear HD video calls. Better patient-physician interactions and accurate visual checks are made possible by this. Real-time sharing of huge medical files, such CT or MRI images, improves diagnosis and treatment planning.

3.1.3. **IoT and Wearable Technology**

3.1.3.1. **Example: Constant Health Monitoring**

- **Situation:** A patient who suffers from a chronic cardiac problem wears a smart device that tracks their blood pressure, heart rate, and other critical indicators all the time.

- **How 5G Is Beneficial:** Through 5G's dependable and quick network, the wearable device transmits real-time data to healthcare providers. Any unusual readings result in instant notifications that let you take appropriate action.

3.1.4. Using Virtual and Augmented Reality in Medical Education:

3.1.4.1. Example: Medical Education Simulations

- **Scenario:** Medical students practice surgery and other medical procedures using AR and VR headsets.
- **How 5G Is Beneficial:** Immersive and responsive AR and VR experiences are made possible by 5G's high bandwidth and low latency. Without having to physically attend a standard training center, students can hone their abilities in dynamic, realistic situations. Collaborative training sessions with professionals from around the globe can also be supported by the technology.

3.1.5. Improved Response Services

3.1.5.1. Example: Ambulance Connectivity:

- **Scenario:** While traveling to the hospital, paramedics in an ambulance transmit real-time patient data and video to the emergency room (ER).
- **How 5G Helps:** By guaranteeing fast and dependable data and video transmission, 5G enables emergency room physicians to plan for patients' arrival and give directives to paramedics while they're on the road. This could potentially save lives by enabling quicker and more efficient treatment during the crucial golden hour.

In summary, because 5G technology will increase the caliber and accessibility of medical services, it will revolutionize the healthcare industry. A wide range of applications, including remote surgeries and enhanced emergency response, are supported by its high-speed, low-latency, and high-capacity capabilities, which ultimately improve patient outcomes and streamline healthcare delivery.

3.2. 5G in Transportation and Smart Cities

5G technology, which offers fast data transfer, low latency, and simultaneous connections across several devices, is essential to the transformation of smart cities and transportation. The following are some thorough illustrations of how 5G is affecting certain industries

3.2.1. **Transportation:**

3.2.1.1. **Transportation**

- **Example: Autonomous Vehicles:**
- **Scenario:** An autonomous vehicle drives through a congested urban area, dodging obstructions and instantly adjusting to traffic signals.
- **How 5G Is Beneficial:** The car's sensors, cameras, and communication systems can process and respond to data nearly instantly thanks to 5G's low latency, which can be as low as 1 millisecond. This is essential for making snap decisions that prevent mishaps. The car's many sensors transmit massive amounts of data to cloud-based systems for sophisticated analysis thanks to the high bandwidth.

3.2.1.2. **Smart Traffic Management:**

- **Example: Intelligent traffic Lights**
- **Scenario:** Based on actual traffic circumstances, traffic lights in a city dynamically modify their timings.
- **How 5G Is Beneficial:** Data on vehicle flow and pedestrian movement is gathered at crossings by sensors and cameras, which transmit the information over a 5G network to a central traffic management system. To ease congestion and enhance traffic flow, the system evaluates the data and modifies the timing of the traffic lights. Both commute times and emissions are decreased by this real-time adjustment.

3.2.1.3. **Improved Public Transportation:**

- **Example: Real-Time Fleet Management**
- **Situation:** A public transportation agency oversees a fleet of buses and makes sure they arrive and depart on time.
- **How 5G Helps:** 5G makes it possible to track buses in real time, giving riders precise ETAs through smartphone apps and digital signage at bus stops. Predictive maintenance and fewer breakdowns are made possible by the high-speed link, which also permits real-time monitoring of bus conditions including fuel levels and engine health.

3.2.2. **Smart Cities**

3.2.2.1. **Smart Grid and Energy Management**

- **Example: Dynamic Energy Distribution**
- **Scenario**: Based on supply and demand in real time, a city's power system dynamically modifies how electricity is distributed.

- **How 5G Is Beneficial:** Real-time data on energy generation and consumption is available across the city thanks to smart meters and other sensors. 5G's dependable and fast link guarantees that this data is examined promptly to optimize energy distribution and cut expenses and waste. Additionally, it makes integrating renewable energy sources easier by compensating for variations in wind and solar output.

3.2.2.2. Smart Waste management

- **Example: Intelligent Waste Collection**
- **Scenario:** Suppose that waste receptacles have sensors that alert them when they are full and require emptying.
- **How 5G Is Beneficial:** Through a 5G network, these sensors transmit real-time data to waste management services. After that, the system schedules waste pickup routes dynamically, maximizing efficiency and minimizing fuel usage. This guarantees prompt disposal of waste and lessens the impact of the waste collecting operation on the environment.

3.2.2.3. Surveillance and Public Safety:

- **Example: Networked Surveillance Cameras**
- **Scenario:** A central security system receives real-time video feeds from surveillance cameras located around the city.
- **How 5G Is Beneficial:** 5G's large bandwidth makes it possible to transmit HD video with next to no latency. These video streams can be processed in real time by advanced analytics to identify anomalous activity, such accidents or crimes, and notify the appropriate authorities right away. Because of this, public safety is improved by permitting faster response times.

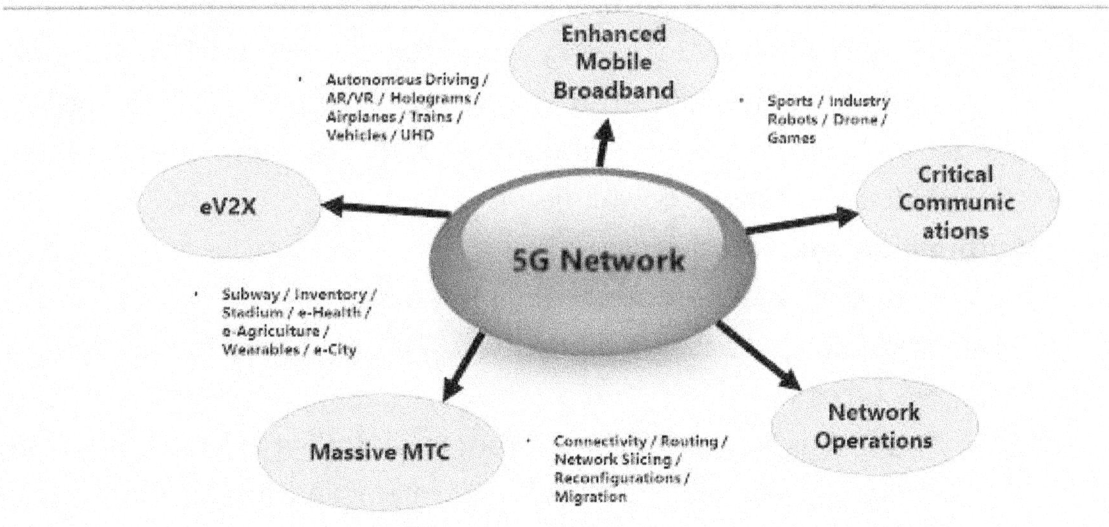

Figure 8: 5G Network - Mission Critical Applications

In summary, 5G technology, which offers the infrastructure required for real-time data sharing, low latency communication, and high device connection, is crucial to the transformation of smart cities and transportation. In the end, these skills contribute to more efficient, safe, and sustainable urban environments. Examples of these breakthroughs include autonomous vehicles, smart traffic management, efficient public transportation, dynamic energy distribution, smart waste management, and improved public safety.

3.3. 5G in Manufacturing and Industry 4.0

Significant improvements in Industry 4.0 and manufacturing are being fueled by 5G technology, which makes it possible to link several devices at once and provides faster, more dependable connectivity as well as increased data transfer capabilities. Here are a few striking illustrations of how 5G is affecting different domains:

3.3.1. Industry 4.0 and Manufacturing:

3.3.1.1. Smart Factories

- **Example: Real-time process control**
- **Scenario:** A factory that makes car parts employs a network of sensors to track and manage manufacturing procedures in real time.

- **How 5G Is Beneficial:** Sensors and control systems can communicate instantly thanks to 5G's low latency. This makes it possible to make adjustments to production lines and machinery in real time, increasing productivity and decreasing waste. Rapid analysis of vast volumes of data from several sensors is made possible by high-speed data communication, which also helps with predictive maintenance and reduces expensive downtime.

3.3.1.2. Automation and Robotics:

- **Example: Autonomous Mobile Robots (AMRs)**
- **Scenario:** In a sizable warehouse, AMRs are utilized to move goods and resources.
- **How 5G Is Beneficial:** These robots can move around the warehouse effectively, avoiding obstacles and interacting in real time with other robots and systems thanks to 5G's high bandwidth and low latency. Even in situations where there is a large density of robotic devices, the capacity to link several devices at once guarantees smooth operation, increasing productivity and lowering operating expenses.

3.3.1.3. Augmented Reality (AR) in Training and Maintenance

- **Example: AR-Assisted Maintenance**
- **Scenario:** To see complex machinery repairs and obtain real-time instructions, maintenance professionals utilize augmented reality headgear.
- **How 5G Is Beneficial:** 5G's fast connectivity makes it possible to send real-time video feeds and intricate 3D models to AR headsets. This minimizes machine downtime and eliminates the need for specialized travel by enabling technicians to obtain professional instruction online. In training scenarios, AR can be used to provide new hires with a controlled, immersive environment in which to practice and learn complex skills.

3.3.1.4. Quality Control and Inspection

- **Example: Automated Quality Inspection**
- **Scenario:** A production line checks products for flaws using high-resolution cameras and sensors.
- **How 5G Is Beneficial:** 5G's high bandwidth enables the quick transfer of sensor and high-resolution picture data to cloud-based artificial

intelligence systems for real-time processing. Imperfect items are promptly detected and eliminated from the manufacturing process, guaranteeing superior quality and minimizing the expenses linked to defective products reaching consumers.

3.3.1.5. Logistics and Supply Chain

- **Example: Real-Time Supply Chain Tracking**
- **Scenario:** A manufacturing corporation monitors the flow of completed goods and raw materials through its supply chain.
- **How 5G Is Beneficial:** 5G-enabled IoT devices and sensors offer real-time data on the position, state, and status of commodities in transit. This helps the business to better manage inventory, streamline operations, and react swiftly to unforeseen events. Costs and delays are minimized because to the supply chain's real-time visibility.

In summary, the foundation of Industry 4.0 and industrial breakthroughs is 5G technology, which offers the infrastructure required for fast, low-latency communication and the capacity to link many devices at once. These features make it possible to create smart factories, boost automation and robots, use augmented reality for maintenance and training, simplify quality control, and maximize supply chain management. As a result, industrial operations become more resilient and efficient while also cutting costs and producing higher-quality goods.

3.4. 5G in Military and Security Operations

5G technology's fast speed, low latency, and extensive networking capabilities promise to transform military and security operations. The following are some significant uses and illustrations of how 5G is being applied in certain domains:

3.4.1. Better Coordination and Communication:

- **Example: Tactical Communications:**
- **How 5G Is Beneficial:** 5G makes it possible for command centers, drones, and soldiers to communicate and share data in real time. This has the potential to significantly increase military operations' effectiveness and responsiveness. For example, soldiers in the field can get real-time updates, maps, and commands straight from their commanders by using augmented reality (AR) glasses connected via 5G. All troops will be synced and able to

quickly adjust to changing battlefield conditions thanks to this improved communication.

3.4.2. Enhanced Reconnaissance and Surveillance:

- **Example: Drone Swarms:**
- **How 5G Is Beneficial:** The military will be able to deploy and control massive drone swarms for surveillance and reconnaissance tasks thanks to 5G. These drones are capable of exchanging real-time sensor data and high-resolution video with one another and a central command center. Drones fitted with cameras and sensors, for instance, can cover a large area during a reconnaissance operation. The captured intelligence enables analysts to make quick choices by transmitting real-time feeds via 5G networks to analysts.

3.4.3. Driverless Cars and Robotics

- **Example: Unmanned aerial vehicles (UAVs) and unmanned ground vehicles (UGVs)**
- **How 5G Is Beneficial:** The deployment of robotics and self-driving cars in military operations is made easier by 5G. These vehicles have low latency whether operated remotely or on their own. To find mines or provide intelligence, for example, an unmanned ground vehicle can be deployed into a dangerous region, greatly lowering the risk to human soldiers. In a similar vein, UAVs can carry out targeted attacks or supply troops in hazardous or isolated areas.

3.4.4. Network Defense and Cybersecurity:

- **Example: Network Slicing for Secure Communications**
- **How 5G Is Beneficial:** The ability to slice a network into separate portions for distinct uses is a feature of 5G that improves security. Critical data flows and communications can be assigned specific network slices in a military setting. This lowers the possibility of cyberattacks and guarantees the security of critical data. A military facility, for instance, might utilize one highly secure network slice for operational instructions and information and another for routine administrative communication.

3.4.5. Improved Simulation and Training:

- **Example: Augmented Reality (AR) and Virtual Reality (VR) Training Courses**

- **How 5G Is Beneficial:** Advanced VR and AR technology can be used for military training thanks to 5G. By participating in incredibly lifelike simulations that replicate real-world events, soldiers can become better equipped for actual combat situations. A soldier could train, for example, in a virtual setting that imitates a particular battlefield down to the dynamic weather and adversary behavior patterns. Compared to conventional techniques, this kind of immersive training—powered by 5G's high bandwidth and low latency—can offer more adaptable and efficient training options.

In summary, there are many benefits to integrating 5G technology into military and security operations, including enhanced communication and real-time data sharing, as well as improved cybersecurity, autonomous vehicle deployment, surveillance, and advanced training techniques. Along with improving operational efficacy and efficiency, these technologies also lead to stronger security protocols and increased military personnel safety. The military and security industries will probably see more and more applications of 5G technology as it develops, substantially altering these domains.

3.5. 5G in Banking and Insurance

Technology improvements, especially with the inclusion of 5G, are driving huge alterations in the banking and insurance sectors. With its extremely quick speeds, minimal latency, and extensive connectivity, this next-generation wireless technology opens up a world of creative applications that can improve security, customer satisfaction, and operational efficiency. Here are some significant effects that 5G is having on these sectors, along with examples:

3.5.1. Improved Client Relationship
- **Example: Real-Time Financial Services:**
- **How 5G Is Beneficial:** Banks and insurance providers will be able to provide real-time services like speedy loan approvals and quick claim processing thanks to 5G. For example, 5G networks' quick data processing and verification capabilities allow a customer to apply for a mortgage and get approved in a matter of minutes. Likewise, real-time processing of insurance

claims enables clients to get information and payouts nearly instantaneously.

3.5.2. Better Mobile Payments and Banking

- **Streamlined Mobile Transactions:**
- **How 5G Is Beneficial:** 5G improves mobile banking by offering connections that are quicker and more dependable, allowing for smoother interactions and transactions. When using mobile apps to make payments, check account balances, or transfer money, customers rarely have to wait. To improve the ease and speed of mobile payments, a user may, for instance, use a mobile wallet app to pay for a coffee. The transaction would be executed nearly instantly.

3.5.3. Personalized Services and Advanced Analytics

- **Example: Financial Advice Driven by AI**
- **How 5G Is Beneficial:** 5G's high-speed connectivity makes it possible to analyze massive amounts of data more successfully by utilizing machine learning (ML) and artificial intelligence (AI). These technologies can be used by banks and insurance providers to provide individualized financial solutions and advice. An AI-powered chatbot, for example, might evaluate a client's spending patterns and financial objectives in real-time and provide the best insurance policies or customized investment advice.

3.5.4. Improved Security and Fraud Identification:

- **Example: Instantaneous Fraud Surveillance**
- **How 5G Is Beneficial:** 5G makes better security measures possible by enabling faster response times and real-time monitoring. Financial institutions can instantly identify and react to fraudulent activity by utilizing advanced artificial intelligence systems. For instance, the bank may tell the consumer right away and temporarily freeze their credit card account if it notices unusual activity. This will stop any more fraudulent transactions.

3.5.5. Integration of the Internet of Things (IoT):

- **Example: Intelligent Insurance Plans:**
- **How 5G Is Beneficial:** 5G can make it easier for IoT devices to be integrated into insurance plans, enabling smarter coverage. For instance, insurers can offer individualized insurance rates based on real-time data

by utilizing data from connected devices like wearables, smart home sensors, and automobile telematics. For homeowners who have Internet of Things (IoT) devices that monitor and notify them of potential threats like fire or water leaks, a smart home insurance coverage may offer reduced premiums.

3.5.6. Telebanking and Remote Branch Services

- **Example: Online Divisions**:
- **How 5G Is Beneficial:** Banks can provide more reliable remote services thanks to 5G, which eliminates the need for physical branches. Via video conferencing and other technological tools, virtual branches can offer a variety of services. For instance, a client in a remote location might use a high-speed 5G connection to virtually meet with a bank representative to create a bank account, apply for a loan, or get financial advice.

3.5.7. Enhanced Risk Management

- **Example: Real-Time Risk Assessment:**
- **How 5G Is Beneficial:** 5G allows real-time data collecting and analysis in the insurance sector, which can enhance risk management and evaluation. For example, insurers can monitor driving behavior and modify premiums based on data from linked automobiles. Insurers are able to better manage their risk portfolios and provide more accurate pricing because to this real-time risk assessment.

In summary, there are several advantages to using 5G in banking and insurance, such as better customer experiences, more security, tailored services, and more effective operations. Financial institutions may innovate and provide more dynamic and responsive services by utilizing 5G's high-speed, low-latency, and huge connection. As 5G technology develops, it will probably have a greater impact on banking and insurance, leading to additional changes in these industries.

3.6. 5G in Retail

The introduction of 5G technology has caused a huge shift in the retail industry. With its high-speed connectivity, low latency, and vast device connectivity, this next-generation wireless technology opens up a world of creative applications that improve customer experience, streamline operations, and open up new business prospects. Here are some significant effects of 5G on the retail sector, along with examples:

3.6.1. **Better In-Store Experience:**
- **Example: Shopping using Augmented Reality (AR)**
- **How 5G Is Beneficial:** 5G makes immersive in-store experiences possible by utilizing augmented reality (AR) technologies. Retailers can give their consumers augmented reality (AR) applications so they can see more information about things in real time or envision the products in their homes. To assist them make more educated purchases, a customer buying furniture, for instance, may use an augmented reality (AR) app to view how a sofa would look in their living room.

3.6.2. **Better Inventory Control:**
- **Real-Time Inventory Monitoring**
- **How 5G Is Beneficial:** Retailers can use 5G to deploy real-time inventory tracking systems that give precise and current stock level information. This can improve inventory control and lessen out-of-stock scenarios. For example, a clothes store may utilize 5G-connected smart shelves and RFID tags to track inventory levels in real-time, making sure that popular goods are always accessible and placing automatic reorders when supplies run low.

3.6.3. Increased Efficiency of the Supply Chain:
- **Smart Logistics:**
- **How 5G Is Beneficial:** 5G technology uses automation and real-time tracking to make supply chain activities more efficient. Retailers may track the location and state of items in transit by using IoT devices connected to 5G networks. To guarantee fresh delivery and minimize wastage, a chain of supermarkets may, for instance, monitor the location and temperature of perishable items as they are being transported.

3.6.4. **Personalised Customer Engagement:**
- **Example: AI-Powered Suggestions**
- **How 5G Is Beneficial:** 5G makes it possible to use artificial intelligence (AI) to deliver individualized shopping experiences more successfully. Retailers can provide personalized product recommendations and promotions by analyzing customer data in real-time. To improve the shopping experience, an online fashion retailer, for example, could utilize artificial intelligence (AI) to examine a customer's past browsing and purchase behavior and offer tailored recommendations and discounts.

3.6.5. Smooth Cross-channel Experiences:

- **Example: Integrated Purchasing Systems**
- **How 5G Is Beneficial:** A unified and consistent consumer experience is offered by 5G's smooth integration of online and offline retail channels. For instance, a consumer may begin their shopping using a store's mobile app, add products to their cart, and finish the transaction without causing any trouble in-store. Retailers may ensure that customers have a seamless and seamless buying experience by using 5G to synchronize data in real-time across all channels.

3.6.6. Advanced Payment Solutions

- **Example: Mobile Wallets and Contactless Payments**
- **How 5G Is Beneficial:** 5G improves contactless payment solutions' speed and security. By providing quicker and more dependable payment methods, retailers can shorten checkout times and increase customer satisfaction. To expedite checkout and decrease wait times, a grocery shop might, for example, install 5G-enabled contactless payment machines that let consumers pay with their smartphones or smartwatches.

3.6.7. Automation and Smart Stores:

- **Example: Self-Driving Robots and Self-Checkout**
- **How 5G Is Beneficial:** 5G makes it easier for automated systems and autonomous robots to be used in retail settings. These robots may help with a variety of jobs, including cleaning, customer service, and shelf replenishing. Robots may be used by a big department store, for instance, to direct consumers to certain products, respond to inquiries, and handle inventory, all of which would improve customer satisfaction and operational effectiveness.

3.6.8. Enhanced Advertising and Marketing:

- **Example: Real-Time Targeted Advertising**
- **How 5G Is Beneficial:** Retailers may offer real-time tailored ads depending on the location and behavior of their customers thanks to 5G. Digital signage connected by 5G, for instance, might be used by a mall to show customers customized advertisements depending on their browsing habits and interests. This focused strategy can boost sales and improve the efficacy of marketing campaigns.

In summary, many benefits arise from the retail industry's adoption of 5G technology, such as improved consumer experiences, more efficient supply chain and inventory management, tailored interaction, and sophisticated payment options. Retailers may innovate and build more dynamic, efficient, and customer-focused operations by utilizing the huge connectivity, low latency, and high speed of 5G. 5G technology's influence on the retail sector will probably rise as it develops, spurring additional change and expansion.

3.7. 5G in Agriculture

Because 5G technology may enable precision farming and improve productivity and sustainability, it has the potential to completely transform the agriculture sector. Here are some significant effects of 5G on agriculture, along with examples:

3.7.1. **Precision Farming**:
- **Example: Smart Irrigation Systems**
- **How 5G Is Beneficial:** The implementation of intelligent irrigation systems that can track soil moisture levels in real-time and modify watering schedules appropriately is made possible by 5G. For example, data from sensors buried in the ground can be sent via a 5G network to a central system that calculates the ideal watering schedule. This encourages healthier crops, uses less water, and yields more.

3.7.2. Data Collection and Real-Time Monitoring
- **Example: Livestock Health Monitoring**
- **How 5G Is Beneficial:** Farmers can utilize IoT devices with 5G to keep an eye on the health and welfare of their cattle. Animals equipped with wearable sensors can monitor their vital signs, movements, and behaviors. This data is then sent to a central platform for study. For instance, the system can notify the farmer right away if a cow exhibits symptoms of illness, enabling timely intervention and lowering the chance of disease spread.

3.7.3. Self-governing Equipment and UAVs
- **Example: Mechanized Planting and Harvesting**
- **How 5G Is Beneficial:** Autonomous equipment can be used for planting, harvesting, and other agricultural operations thanks to 5G. With the aid of real-time data, these devices are capable of extremely precise and efficient operation. To maximize crop density and raise production, a self-driving tractor

with 5G connectivity, for instance, can sow seeds at specific depths and intervals. Drones can also be used to check agricultural health, capture overhead photographs, and spray fertilizer or insecticides.

3.7.4. Better Crop Management:

- **Example: Real-Time Crop Monitoring:**
- **How 5G Is Beneficial:** 5G enables drones and sensors to continuously monitor agricultural conditions. These gadgets are able to gather information on a number of variables, including temperature, humidity, pest activity, and soil health. For example, a network of sensors can identify the first indications of a pest infestation and notify the farmer, enabling him to take focused action to contain the issue before it becomes worse.

3.7.5. Enhanced Supply Chain Effectiveness:

- **Example: Traceability and Transparency**
- **How 5G Is Beneficial:** Throughout the supply chain, 5G can enhance the agricultural products' transparency and traceability. Real-time produce tracking from farm to table gives consumers comprehensive knowledge about the source and path of their food. To ensure quality and safety, a farm could, for instance, use 5G-connected sensors to monitor the circumstances surrounding the harvest, storage, and transportation of fruit. To foster trust and guarantee adherence to legal requirements, this information might be made available to shops and customers.

3.7.6. Enhanced Decision Making:

- **Example: Predictive Analytics with AI and Machine Learning**
- **How 5G Is Beneficial:** 5G makes it easier to evaluate vast amounts of agricultural data and produce insightful conclusions by utilizing AI and machine learning. Predictive analytics, for example, can assist farmers in allocating resources, scheduling plantings, and rotating crops in an educated manner. To maximize productivity and lower risks, an AI system may suggest the ideal times to plant and harvest crops based on analysis of historical yield data, weather patterns, and soil conditions.

3.7.7. Sustainable Agriculture Practices

- **Example: Precision Fertilization**
- **How 5G Is Beneficial:** Farmers can use 5G to lower their farming's environmental effect by using precise fertilizing techniques. Fertilizers may be applied precisely where needed by using sensors and drones to evaluate plant

health and soil nutrient levels. As a result, less chemicals are used, less runoff pollutes water sources, and more environmentally friendly farming methods are encouraged.

3.7.8. Remote Control and Management

- **Example: Remote Maintenance and Monitoring**
- **How 5G Is Beneficial:** Farmers can oversee and control their operations remotely from any location thanks to 5G. For instance, a farmer could monitor cattle, assess the condition of irrigation systems, and get notifications about equipment failures using a smartphone or tablet. This remote capacity can help farmers maintain efficient operations and solve problems quickly by saving time and resources.

In summary, enhancing precision farming, real-time monitoring, autonomous machinery, increased supply chain efficiency, and sustainable practices are just a few advantages of integrating 5G technology in agriculture. Farmers can streamline their processes, boost output, and support environmental sustainability by utilizing 5G's high speed, low latency, and extensive connectivity. The impact of 5G technology on agriculture is expected to grow as it develops, spurring additional innovation and industry revolution.

3.8.   5G in Education and Training

5G technology, which offers fast, dependable, low-latency connectivity, is poised to revolutionize training and education. This change makes better teaching techniques, increased accessibility, and improved learning experiences possible. Here are some significant effects of 5G on training and education, along with examples:

3.8.1. Improved Experiences with Augmented and Virtual Reality (VR/AR)

- **Example: Interactive Science Classes**
- **How 5G Is Beneficial:** Applications for VR and AR can be used in classrooms more successfully with 5G. For instance, biology students studying virtual reality headsets can examine a human body in three dimensions, viewing organs and systems up close and engaging with them in ways that are not feasible in a conventional classroom. An immersive experience like this can improve learning's intuitiveness and engagement.

3.8.2. Real-Time Collaboration and Interactive Learning:

- **Example: Remote Classroom Participation**

- **How 5G Is Beneficial:** 5G makes it possible for students to engage in class from anywhere in the world with real-time, high-quality video conferencing. To close the achievement gap, kids in underprivileged or rural areas can attend virtual classrooms where they can engage in real-time interactions with their teachers and peers. Additionally, it makes it easier for students to collaborate on assignments and projects in real-time, regardless of where they are physically located.

3.8.3. Personalised Educational Opportunities

- **Example: Adaptive Learning Platforms**
- **How 5G Is Beneficial:** 5G facilitates the deployment of AI-powered adaptive learning systems that customize course material to meet the needs of specific students. An online learning platform, for instance, has the ability to evaluate a student's performance in real time and modify the content's difficulty by offering extra help or practice questions. The ability for each student to study at their own pace and style is facilitated by this individualized approach.

3.8.4. Enhanced Accessibility:

- **Example: Inclusive Education for Students with Disabilities**
- **How 5G Is Beneficial:** For students with impairments, 5G can significantly increase accessibility. To facilitate the participation of students with hearing impairments in live classes, real-time captioning and sign language interpreting services can be offered. Furthermore, from the comfort of their homes, students with mobility impairments can engage in virtual classes and access the same educational resources.

3.8.5. Effective Operations Management and Administration:

- **Example: Smart Campuses**
- **How 5G Is Beneficial:** 5G has the potential to turn learning environments into smart campuses where IoT devices oversee numerous functions. For instance, real-time monitoring and management of energy consumption by sensors can lower expenses and increase sustainability. Access control systems and 5G-connected cameras can improve security, guaranteeing a secure atmosphere for employees and students.

3.8.6. Improved Education and Career Growth:

- **Example: Virtual Reality Simulations for Medical Training**
- **How 5G Is Beneficial:** 5G makes it possible for complex simulations to be used in professional training, giving students practical experience without the

hazards. For example, medical students can practice procedures with high-fidelity virtual reality simulations of real-world circumstances. The training experience is improved overall by these simulations, which offer quick feedback and can be repeated as needed to increase expertise.

3.8.7. **Expanded Research and Data Analysis:**
   - **Example: Collaborative Research Projects**
   - **How 5G Is Beneficial:** Large-scale collaborative research initiatives are made easier by 5G's ability to share and analyze massive datasets seamlessly. For instance, experts from various institutions can collaborate on challenging scientific challenges and share data and findings in real time without experiencing lag. This increases the effectiveness and reach of research initiatives.

3.8.8. **Gamification of Education:**
   - **Example: Interactive Educational Games**
   - **How 5G Is Beneficial:** The creation of interactive, high-quality learning games that make learning enjoyable and interesting is supported by 5G. An interactive history game that lets pupils "time travel" and experience historical events would be a useful tool for a history teacher. Students' motivation and information retention may rise as a result of these gamified learning opportunities.

In summary, many advantages come with using 5G technology into training and education programs, such as more immersive learning environments, instantaneous collaboration, customized instruction, increased accessibility, and effective operational management. Through the utilization of 5G's dependable, fast, and low-latency connectivity, training providers and educational institutions may create more inclusive, productive, and engaging learning environments. The impact of 5G technology on training and education will probably increase as it develops, spurring more innovation and change in these areas.

3.9. 5G in Smart Homes

5G technology's high-speed, low-latency, and dependable connectivity have the potential to greatly improve smart home systems. Convenience, security, and energy management are all enhanced by this breakthrough, which makes home automation more effective, responsive, and integrated. Here are some significant effects of 5G on smart homes, along with examples:

3.9.1. **Improved Connectivity and Device Integration:**
- **Example: Seamless Smart Device Integration**
- **How 5G Is Beneficial:** 5G makes it possible for a wide range of smart home products, security cameras, lights, and thermostats to integrate and connect seamlessly. For instance, a homeowner can ensure that all of their smart gadgets function harmoniously by controlling them all from a single interface, such as a smartphone app or a smart home hub. Complex automation situations, such as locking doors, adjusting the thermostat, and turning off lights when the homeowner leaves the house, are made possible by this integration.

3.9.2. **Better Home Security Systems**
- **Example: Real-Time Surveillance and Alerts**
- **How 5G Is Beneficial:** Instant warnings and high-resolution, real-time video surveillance are two ways that 5G improves home security systems. For example, homeowners can watch their property remotely in real-time with minimal latency when using smart security cameras connected via 5G. The homeowner's smartphone can receive immediate warnings from the system in the event of any odd activity, allowing for prompt action in the event of a security danger.

3.9.3. Advanced Energy Management
- **Example: Smart Energy Grids and Appliances**
- **How 5G Is Beneficial:** 5G makes real-time monitoring and control of energy consumption possible, which makes advanced energy management possible. For instance, smart appliances can be programmed to run during off-peak hours to save energy expenses, and smart meters can offer comprehensive insights into patterns of energy consumption. By using this information, homeowners may optimize their energy use and help create a more economical and environmentally friendly home.

3.9.4. **Improved Entertainment Systems**
- **Example: Cloud Gaming with 4K/8K Streaming**
- **How 5G Is Beneficial:** 5G offers improved entertainment through supporting high-bandwidth applications like cloud gaming and 4K/8K video streaming. For

example, gamers can enjoy cloud-based gaming services with minimum latency, and smart TVs can broadcast material in ultra-high resolution without buffering. This feature guarantees that no one in the family will have to sacrifice performance to enjoy top-notch entertainment at the same time.

3.9.5. Health and Wellness Monitoring

- **Example: Connected Health Devices**
- **How 5G Is Beneficial:** The smart home ecosystem can now include health and wellness devices thanks to 5G. Smart wearables and health monitoring devices, for instance, are capable of continually monitoring vital signs including blood pressure, heart rate, and sleep habits. To improve individual health management, this data can be sent in real-time to healthcare providers for remote monitoring and early health issue detection.

3.9.6. AI Integration with Voice-Activated Assistants:

- **Smart Assistants with Enhanced Features**
- **How 5G Is Beneficial:** Voice-activated assistants such as Apple Siri, Google Assistant, and Amazon Alexa operate better with 5G. These intelligent assistants are able to control a larger variety of smart devices, react to voice instructions more quickly, and deliver information that is more accurate. For example, a homeowner can use voice control to launch a sophisticated automation routine, such "Good Morning," which updates the weather, adjusts the lighting, and starts the coffee maker.

3.9.7. Improved Automation and Remote Control:

- **Example: Remote Home Management**
- **How 5G Is Beneficial:** Smart home system remote control is now more rapid and dependable thanks to 5G. For example, homeowners can use their smartphone or tablet to remotely change the lighting, temperature, and security settings of their home from anywhere in the world. This feature is very helpful for maintaining holiday rentals or making sure the house is comfortable when guests arrive.

3.9.8. Smart Kitchen and Appliances

- **Example: Networked Kitchen Appliances**
- **How 5G Is Beneficial:** Smarter kitchen equipment with remote control and monitoring are made possible by 5G. For instance, a smart oven may be remotely prepared to guarantee supper is ready on time, and a refrigerator can track its contents and recommend dishes depending on ingredients that are

available. The efficiency and convenience of the kitchen are improved by these networked gadgets.

In summary, there are several advantages to integrating 5G technology into smart homes, such as better security, increased connectivity, sophisticated energy management, and more enjoyable entertainment. Through the utilization of 5G's dependable, fast, and low-latency connectivity, homeowners may design smart home solutions that are more effective, responsive, and integrated. The impact of 5G technology on smart homes is expected to grow as it develops, spurring additional innovation and changing our way of life.

3.10. 5G in Waste Management

5G technology's high-speed, low-latency, and dependable connectivity have the potential to greatly improve waste management systems. Waste management techniques could become more effective, efficient, and sustainable as a result of this development. Here are some significant effects of 5G on waste management, along with examples:

3.10.1.   Smart Waste Cans and Sensors
- **Example: Real-Time Fill Level Monitoring**
- The usage of intelligent trash cans with sensors that track fill levels in real time is made possible by 5G. For example, sensors installed in public trash cans can communicate with a central management system via a 5G network to provide information on when the cans should be emptied. Waste collection agencies can use this data to improve their routes, ensuring that bins are emptied only when necessary, saving gasoline and increasing efficiency.

3.10.2. **Optimised Waste Collection Routes**
- **Example: Dynamic Route Planning**
- 5G enables dynamic route planning by facilitating real-time communication between central management systems and waste collection vehicles. For instance, collection routes can be dynamically modified to minimize travel distances and prevent traffic congestion based on real-time data from smart garbage bins. This lowers operating expenses and carbon emissions while also saving time and gasoline.

3.10.3. **Improved Procedures for Sorting and Recycling**
- **Example: Automated Sorting Facilities**

- Through machine-to-machine connection and real-time data sharing, 5G facilitates the automation of recycling and sorting operations. For instance, intelligent sorting devices with 5G connectivity can instantly identify and classify various trash kinds through the use of artificial intelligence and cutting-edge photography. As a result, sorting becomes more precise and efficient, raising recycling rates and lowering contamination in recycling streams.

3.10.4. Predictive Maintenance of Waste Management Equipment

- **Example: Real-Time Equipment Monitoring**
- By allowing for real-time monitoring of waste management machinery like garbage trucks and compactors, 5G makes predictive maintenance possible. Sensors can monitor the performance and operating state of machinery, providing maintenance crews with data. For example, the hydraulic system of a garbage truck can notify maintenance staff to service the truck before it breaks down, reducing repair costs and downtime.

3.10.5. Better Handling of Hazardous Waste:

- **Example: Real-Time Monitoring of Hazardous Materials**
- Hazardous waste products can now be tracked and monitored in real time thanks to 5G. For instance, sensors that track variables like temperature, pressure, and location can be installed in containers carrying hazardous trash. To guarantee that hazardous items are handled and disposed of safely, lowering the risk of accidents and environmental damage, this data can be communicated across 5G networks.

3.10.6. Better Public Services and Citizen Involvement:

- **Example: Waste Management Mobile Apps**
- The creation of smartphone apps that improve public participation in garbage management is supported by 5G. For example, people can report illegal dumping, overflowing dumpsters, and missed pickups using apps. Real-time processing of these reports enables waste management services to react quickly. Apps can also offer details about recycling policies and timetables, which promotes more conscientious trash disposal practices.

3.10.7. Smart Landfills:

- **Example: Environmental Monitoring**
- By monitoring the environment, 5G can help manage landfills more effectively. Landfills can have sensors installed inside and outside to track things like ground stability, leachate levels, and gas emissions. For instance, landfill

operators can reduce environmental effects by taking prompt action to capture and turn methane into electricity with the use of real-time data on methane gas emissions.

3.10.8.   Data-Driven Decision Making:

- **Example: Advanced Analytics for Waste Management**
- Large-scale data collection and analysis from multiple sources inside the waste management ecosystem is made possible by 5G. To spot patterns and improve operations, data from smart bins, collection trucks, and recycling facilities, for instance, can be reviewed. By offering insights into waste generation trends, advanced analytics can assist businesses and localities in creating waste reduction plans that are more successful.

In summary, there are many advantages to integrating 5G technology into trash management, such as enhanced hazardous waste management, better public participation, recycling processes that are optimized, real-time monitoring, and predictive maintenance. Utilizing 5G's fast, dependable, low-latency connectivity, waste management systems can become more responsive, sustainable, and efficient. The impact of 5G technology on waste management is expected to increase as it develops, spurring additional innovation and industry transformation.

Chapter 4: 5G and the Internet of Things (IoT)

The Internet of Things (IoT) and 5G are closely related technologies that will revolutionize a number of industries by making the world more efficient and connected. An outline of each and their connection is provided below:

The fifth generation of cellular network technology, or 5G, provides a number of significant improvements over 4G.

4.1.1. **Greater Speeds:** Compared to 4G, 5G can deliver data speeds of up to 10 Gbps, which is a huge increase.

4.1.2. **Reduced Latency:** 5G networks have latency as low as 1 millisecond, which increases the viability of real-time applications and communication.

4.1.3. **Enhanced Capacity:** 5G has the capacity to accommodate more devices per unit space, which is essential for Internet of Things applications.

4.1.4. **Enhanced Reliability:** 5G is perfect for sensitive applications because of its improved reliability and decreased interference.

4.1.5. **Network Slicing:** This feature enables the development of several virtual networks within of a single 5G physical network, providing specialized solutions for various uses.

The term "Internet of Things" (IoT) describes a network of actual objects, including cars, appliances, and other household equipment, that are implanted with sensors, software, and connection. This allows the objects to communicate with one another and share data.

4.2.1. **Connected Devices:** The Internet of Things (IoT) encompasses a wide range of gadgets, from industrial gear to home appliances.

4.2.2. **Data Collection:** By gathering and transmitting data, these technologies allow for automation and insightful analysis.

4.2.3. **Applications:** There are numerous uses for IoT, including smart homes, manufacturing, transportation, healthcare, and agriculture.

4.2.4. **Automation and Control:** IoT makes it possible to monitor and control remotely, which boosts convenience and efficiency.

The synergy between 5G and IoT is especially potent, propelling advancements and augmenting capacities in multiple ways:

4.3.1. **Enhanced Connectivity:** 5G's rapid speed and low latency are critical for Internet of Things (IoT) devices to function seamlessly, particularly in applications that demand real-time data processing and reaction.

4.3.2. **Massive Device Support:** 5G's capacity to handle a vast array of IoT devices is essential for use in industrial and smart city applications.

4.3.3. **Enhanced Reliability:** 5G networks' increased dependability guarantees dependable operation for vital Internet of Things applications like driverless cars and healthcare.

4.3.4. **Energy Efficiency:** 5G technologies are intended to use less energy, which is advantageous for Internet of Things devices that run on batteries.

4.3.5. **New Use Cases:** The combination of 5G and IoT opens up new possibilities for use cases like self-driving cars, remote surgery, smart grids, and more. Utilization Examples

4.3.6. **Smart Cities:** Combining gadgets and sensors to control energy use, traffic, and public safety.

4.3.7. **Healthcare:** Smart medical equipment, telemedicine, and remote monitoring.

4.3.8. **Manufacturing**: Improved supply chain management, automated production lines, and predictive maintenance.

4.3.9. **Agriculture**: automated irrigation systems, livestock monitoring, and precision farming.

4.3.10. **Transportation:** networked infrastructure, intelligent traffic control, and driverless cars.

To summarise, the amalgamation of 5G and IoT signifies a noteworthy progression in connectivity and technical innovation, holding the potential to revolutionise various industries and enhance efficacy, security, and standard of living in several aspects.

The phrase *"Connecting the Unconnected"* describes initiatives to give people and places that do not already have connectivity access to the internet. Ensuring digital inclusion and promoting social, educational, and economic prospects depend heavily on this project.

The way we live and work is changing due to the Internet of Things (IoT), which is a network of interconnected "smart" gadgets that communicate easily via the Internet. Wireless Internet of Things sensors on farms may send data on nutrients and soil moisture to agricultural specialists around the nation. Long-term safety for homeowners is offered by Internet of Things alarm systems, which come with long-lasting batteries. Both humans and pets can use wearable fitness gadgets to track their activity levels and receive heart rate and breathing data.

Despite the fact that these apps have various functions, they are all dependent on reliable internet. IoT vendors and chipset manufacturers, radio and chipset manufacturers, device manufacturers, and businesses from a range of industries that buy IoT-enabled goods for their own use or to sell to the general public are among the stakeholders in the IoT space looking for connection solutions. These businesses now have access to over thirty distinct connectivity alternatives, each with varying capabilities for network management, pricing, dependability, bandwidth, and range.

This great diversity, along with the ever-changing demands of technology, leads to a dilemma. Stakeholders' IoT applications, devices, and solutions may quickly become outdated if they place bets on one connectivity option and another emerges as the winner. They risk losing ground to more assertive rivals if they wait to observe how the connectivity scene develops. The following are important tactics and illustrations of how to do this:

4.4.1. Infrastructure Development

- **Fiber Optic Networks:** High-speed internet connectivity can be obtained in rural and isolated places by installing and extending fiber optic cables. For instance, fiber optic connections have been installed in Uganda as part of Google's Project Link to increase connectivity and internet speeds.

- **Mobile Networks:** Access may be greatly increased by extending 3G, 4G, and now 5G networks into less connected areas. In India, Reliance Jio has raised internet penetration by offering 4G LTE services at a reasonable price.

4.4.2. Satellite Internet

- **Low Earth Orbit (LEO) satellites:** Organizations such as SpaceX, through its Starlink initiative, are putting constellations of LEO satellites into orbit to offer worldwide internet access, even in underserved and isolated places. High-speed internet can be provided via this technology in locations where running cables is impractical.
- **Geostationary Satellites:** Although they have a larger latency than LEO satellites, traditional satellite internet providers like Viasat and HughesNet provide connection in rural and isolated areas.

4.4.3. Community Networks:

- **Local Cooperatives and ISPs:** In many areas, community cooperatives and local internet service providers construct and run their own networks. For instance, Guifi.net, a sizable community network in Spain, offers internet access using a decentralized, neighborhood-driven architecture.
- **Mesh Networks:** These networks weave a web of connected devices that share internet access together using local nodes. One example is NYC Mesh, where volunteers install nodes to bring internet access to underserved sections of the city.

4.4.4. Public Hotspots and Wi-Fi

- **Municipal Wi-Fi:** Cities such as San Francisco and Barcelona provide free public Wi-Fi in a number of areas, giving people who would not be able to purchase personal connections access to the internet.
- **Rural Hotspots:** Organizations in nations like Kenya have installed Wi-Fi hotspots in rural areas to provide access to the internet for business and educational purposes.

4.4.5. Innovative Technologies

- **TV White Space:** This technology provides internet connectivity by using underutilized TV spectrum broadcasting frequencies. Through TV white spaces, Microsoft's Airband Initiative offers connectivity to rural areas of Africa and America.
- **Balloon-Based Networks:** To build an aerial wireless network, Alphabet's Project Loon uses high-altitude balloons. This concept has been implemented

in areas hit by natural disasters or lacking infrastructure, as Puerto Rico following Hurricane Maria.

4.4.6. Government and Policy Support

- **Subsidies and Incentives:** To encourage ISPs to expand service to disconnected areas, governments might provide them with financial incentives and subsidies. The Connect America Fund of the US FCC helps underserved communities implement broadband.
- **Universal Service Funds (USFs):** To support communications services in underserved and rural areas, numerous nations have set up USFs. One example is the FUNTTEL fund in Brazil, which aims to increase telecom infrastructure.

4.4.7. Outreach and Education Initiatives

- **Digital Literacy Training:** It's critical to educate people on how to use digital technologies and the internet. The goal of initiatives like India's Digital Saksharta Abhiyan (DISHA) is to increase the digital literacy of one member of each family.
- **Access to Gadgets:** By guaranteeing that people have the means to access to the internet, programs like the One Laptop per Child project that aim to provide inexpensive or free gadgets aid in closing the gap.

4.4.8. Collaborative Efforts and Partnerships

- **Public-Private Partnerships (PPPs):** These alliances allow governments, non-profit organizations, and private businesses to combine resources and knowledge. One instance is the partnership on Project Loon that exists between Google, Telkom Kenya, and the Kenyan government.
- **NGO and Corporate Initiatives:** Projects to enhance worldwide internet access are undertaken by groups such as the Internet Society and companies such as Facebook, which operates the Connectivity Lab (a division of Internet.org).

4.4.9. Impacts and Examples

4.4.9.1. **Education:** Students in Peru now have access to a wider variety of online learning platforms and educational resources thanks to the installation of internet in distant institutions.

4.4.9.2. **Healthcare:** Where there is inadequate infrastructure for healthcare, telemedicine services have emerged as a feasible option for providing necessary medical consultations and services in remote regions of Africa.

4.4.9.3.   **Economic Growth:** Farmers in rural India can now check weather forecasts and market prices thanks to internet connection, which has increased agricultural output and income.

We can close the digital divide and promote more inclusion and equal chances in the digital age by connecting the disconnected.

Chapter 5: The Future of Mobile Communication

One of the main applications of 5G technology is *Enhanced Mobile Broadband* (eMBB), which is a major advancement over 4G LTE. In high-density locations, *eMBB promises to deliver significantly quicker data speeds, increased capacity, and an enhanced user experience*. The main points and instances that highlight eMBB's influence and future possibilities for mobile communication are provided below.

5.1.1. Improving User Experience in Congested Spaces

- **Example: Sporting Events and Concerts**
- Congestion is a common issue for existing networks at large-scale events involving thousands of attendees. *High user densities will be supported by eMBB, guaranteeing uninterrupted social media access, live streaming, and video sharing for all users*. Envision being at a crowded stadium where you can instantly post videos to social media.

5.1.2. Enhanced Connectivity in City Settings

- **Example: Smart Cities**
- Strong connectivity for applications like high-definition surveillance, smart traffic management, and improved public services will be made possible by eMBB in smart cities. For instance, quick and dependable data transfer is needed for high-resolution cameras installed across a city in order to efficiently monitor and control urban infrastructure.

5.1.3. Augmented Reality (AR) and Virtual Reality (VR)

- **Example: Immersive Experiences**
- High bandwidth and low latency are required for AR and VR applications, and eMBB can deliver both. This will change distant work, gaming, and education. For example, virtual reality gaming is expected to enhance its immersion and interactivity, while virtual classrooms can provide authentic, real-time interactions between educators and learners.

5.1.4. Improved Mobile Workforces:

- **Example: Remote Collaboration and Work**
- Remote work will significantly improve using eMBB. Cloud computing, real-time collaboration on massive files, and high-quality video

conferencing will all be more effective. Clearer video calls and faster data sharing will be made possible by platforms like Zoom and Microsoft Teams, facilitating more productive distant team collaboration.

5.1.5. Internet of Things and Wearable Devices:

- **Example: Health Monitoring**
- eMBB will help the growth of wearables and IoT devices. Healthcare professionals will be able to monitor patients continuously and take prompt action thanks to the real-time data that wearable health monitors will send. Smartwatches, for instance, will provide physicians with high-fidelity health indicators, facilitating improved patient care.

5.1.6. Strengthened Emergency Services and Public Safety

- **Real-Time Incident Response**
- By giving emergency responders access to real-time data, eMBB will improve public safety. During emergencies, control centers can get instantaneous high-definition video feeds from drones or body cameras, which enhances situational awareness and response times.

5.1.7. Rural Connectivity

- **Example: Bridging the Digital Divide:**
- By extending high-speed internet to underserved and rural areas, eMBB can close the digital divide. For example, distant areas would have access to digital services like telemedicine and online education that were previously unattainable because of network issues.

In summary, improved Mobile Broadband (eMBB) promises to transform mobile communication with its increased capacity, quicker data speeds, and better application user experiences. eMBB will be crucial in determining how mobile connectivity develops in the future, since it will enable immersive AR/VR experiences, support smart city infrastructure, broadcast ultra-high quality content, and improve remote work. Its effects will be seen in a variety of industries, raising standards of living, productivity, and accessibility everywhere.

5.2. Ultra-Reliable Low Latency Communication (URLLC)

Another important pillar of 5G technology is *Ultra-Reliable Low Latency Connectivity* (URLLC), which *focuses on providing incredibly low-latency and highly reliable connectivity*. Applications that demand great dependability and real-time data transmission must have this capacity. These are some salient features and illustrations of URLLC's potential and impact on mobile communication in the future.

5.2.1. Autonomous Cars

- **Example: Self-Driving Cars**
- Real-time data is essential for autonomous cars to make snap choices. Cars may connect with traffic signals, road infrastructure, and other vehicles thanks to *Vehicle-to-Everything* (V2X) communication, which is supported by URLLC's low latency and high dependability. For example, a self-driving automobile can react immediately when it receives notifications regarding traffic conditions or road hazards.

5.2.2. Robotics and Industrial Automation:

- **Example: Smart Factories as an Example Cars**
- Robots and other machinery in smart factories must be able to interact quickly with one another and with central control systems. By ensuring that data and commands are sent in real-time, URLLC lowers downtime and boosts productivity. For instance, robotic arms in an auto assembly line may precisely coordinate their movements to assemble parts quickly, boosting output and lowering mistakes.

5.2.3. Medical Care and Virtual Surgery:

- **Example: Telesurgery**
- Enabling remote operations and other vital medical procedures is one way that URLLC can transform the healthcare industry. Using robotic equipment operated in real time, surgeons can do remote operations on patients. For example, a surgeon in New York may operate on a patient in a distant part of Africa while receiving real-time haptic input and video, guaranteeing accuracy and dependability much like they would if they were there in person.

5.2.4. Monitoring of Critical Infrastructure:

- **Example: Power Grid Management**
- Ultra-reliable and low-latency communication is necessary for controlling and monitoring vital infrastructure, such as transportation networks, water supply systems, and power grids. Faults or anomalies can be immediately detected and responded to with URLLC. For instance, URLLC makes sure that the control center is informed

immediately in the event that a power grid sensor detects a defect, enabling prompt corrective action to avert blackouts.

5.2.5. Public Safety and Emergency Services

- **Example: Disaster Response**
- Reliable and low-latency communication is essential for public safety and rescue operations coordination in emergency situations. Drones, control centers, and emergency responders may share data in real time thanks to URLLC. Drones with cameras and sensors, for example, can give rescue teams real-time video feeds during a natural disaster, which can assist them find survivors and organize effective rescue efforts.

5.2.6. Virtual Reality (VR) and Augmented Reality (AR)

- **Example: Real-Time AR/VR Applications**
- By guaranteeing that data is transferred with the least amount of latency, URLLC improves AR and VR experiences. This is important for applications such as virtual tours, gaming, and remote training. For instance, real-time augmented reality overlays can help technicians in remote training sessions for complex machinery by guiding them through the repair procedure in real time, thus increasing accuracy and efficiency.

5.2.7. Financial Trading

- **Example: High-Frequency Trading**
- Milliseconds can have a big impact on trade in the financial sector. High-frequency trading platforms need low latency to process transactions quickly, and URLLC offers that. In order to optimize their tactics for higher returns, traders can respond to market movements faster than their rivals when they use algorithmic trading systems.

5.2.8. Energy Management and Smart Grid

- **Example: Real-Time Energy Distribution**
- By enabling real-time communication between multiple smart grid components, URLLC can optimize the distribution of energy. For instance, the grid can dynamically alter power distribution during peak hours to balance the load and avoid outages, guaranteeing a reliable and effective energy supply.

In summary, when it comes to essential applications, Ultra-Reliable Low Latency Communication (URLLC) is going to revolutionize a number of industries by offering the high reliability and low latency needed. URLLC will be crucial to the advancement of technology and the efficiency, safety, and dependability of many systems. It will enable driverless vehicles, industrial automation, medical remote surgery, and public safety during emergencies. It will have a significant impact on many other sectors, spurring innovation and opening up new opportunities.

5.3. Massive Machine Type Communication (mMTC)

One of the most important aspects of 5G technology is *Massive Machine Type Communication (mMTC), which is intended to facilitate the widespread networking of IoT devices.* Even with little assistance from humans, billions of devices can connect and communicate effectively thanks to mMTC. This feature is *essential for many applications that depend on widely dispersed sensor networks and Internet of Things devices.* These are some of the main points and instances that highlight the influence and possibilities of mMTC on mobile communication in the future.

5.3.1. Smart Cities

- **Example: Urban Infrastructure Management**
- By enabling the widespread deployment of IoT devices in urban settings, mMTC improves the infrastructure of smart cities. Public transit systems, garbage management, traffic conditions, and air quality can all be observed by sensors. For instance, sensor-equipped smart streetlights can change their brightness according to the time of day and foot traffic.

5.3.2. Autonomous Cars

- **Example: Self-Driving Cars**
- Real-time data is essential for autonomous cars to make snap choices. Cars may connect with traffic signals, road infrastructure, and other vehicles thanks to vehicle-to-everything (V2X) communication, which is supported by URLLC's low latency and high dependability. For example, a self-driving automobile can react immediately when it receives notifications regarding traffic conditions or road hazards.

5.3.3. Agriculture

- **Example: Precision Farming**

- Precision farming techniques in agriculture are made possible by mMTC, which links an extensive range of sensors and equipment to track crop health, weather patterns, soil conditions, and irrigation systems. For example, farmers may optimize watering schedules and save water usage while increasing crop yields by using real-time data from soil moisture sensors.

5.3.4. Environmental Monitoring

- **Example: Tracking and Conserving Wildlife**
- By placing sensors in far-off and varied places to monitor wildlife movements, forest health, and water quality, mMTC makes environmental monitoring easier. For instance, sensors affixed to animals can yield information about their migratory patterns, which aids in the development of conservationists' strategies for safeguarding threatened species and their environments.

5.3.5. Healthcare

- **Example: Remote Patient Monitoring**
- mMTC makes it possible for wearable technology and remote monitoring systems to be widely used in the healthcare industry to track patients' health conditions in real time. Wearable technology, for example, can track blood pressure, glucose levels, and heart rate. It can then send this information to medical professionals, who can quickly take appropriate action if any irregularities are found.

5.3.6. Manufacturing

- **Example: Industrial IoT (IIoT)**
- By connecting a sizable network of sensors and machinery inside plants, mMTC facilitates Industrial IoT (IIoT) in the manufacturing sector. Production process automation and real-time monitoring are made possible by this link. On assembly lines, for instance, sensors can identify quality problems or equipment failures, allowing for quick corrections and reduced downtime.

5.3.7. Supply Chain and Logistics Management

- **Example: Tracking Assets**
- mMTC offers real-time asset and inventory tracking, which facilitates effective supply chain management and logistics. For example, sensors affixed to shipping containers have the ability to track their position,

temperature, and humidity, guaranteeing the timely and safe delivery of goods—particularly perishables.

5.3.8. Energy and Utilities

- **Examples: Smart Grids**
- In order to monitor and control the distribution of energy, smart grids, which depend on a multitude of sensors and devices, are developed with the help of mMTC. For instance, utility firms may optimize energy distribution and cut waste by using real-time energy usage data from smart meters installed in homes and businesses.

5.3.9. Transportation

- **Example: Vehicle Connectivity**
- When it comes to transportation, mMTC makes it possible to use connected vehicle technologies, which let cars talk to each other and the road infrastructure. For instance, data sharing between traffic lights and car sensors can optimize traffic flow, lessen congestion, and increase road safety.

In summary, through enabling large-scale connectivity of IoT devices, Massive Machine Type Communication, or mMTC, has the potential to change a number of industries. mMTC will spur innovation and efficiency in a variety of fields, including precision farming, smart city infrastructure, remote monitoring for improved healthcare, and logistics and energy management optimization. It will have a big impact on building smarter, more connected settings, which will boost economic growth, sustainability, and quality of life.

Chapter 6: Economic and Social Impacts of 5G

6.1. The Economic Benefits of 5G

The Economic Advantages of 5G, or fifth generation mobile network technology, is *expected to completely transform many different economic sectors*. Its economic advantages can be roughly divided into direct and indirect effects, each of which has a major positive impact on the expansion of the world economy.

6.1.1. Enhanced Productivity

5G's low latency and high-speed connectivity boost productivity in a number of industries:

- **Manufacturing:** 5G networks are used in smart factories to link machines and sensors, enabling automation and real-time monitoring. For instance, 5G-enabled predictive maintenance can lower maintenance expenses and downtime. Businesses such as Bosch are integrating 5G technology into their factories to enhance their production lines and track the condition of their equipment, leading to more effective operations.
- **Healthcare:** Real-time data sharing, remote surgery, and telemedicine are made possible with 5G. Robotic technologies allow surgeons to operate from a distance. The usage of telehealth services enabled by 5G technology increased during the COVID-19 epidemic, offering vital care in remote locations and lessening the strain on medical facilities.

6.1.2. Job Creation and Economic Growth

An important economic stimulus is the rollout of 5G infrastructure itself:

- **Network Expansion:** The development and maintenance of 5G networks necessitate large infrastructural investments, generating employment in the building, engineering, and telecommunications sectors. For example, multi-billion dollar investments in 5G deployment have been announced by AT&T and Verizon, which boosts economic activity and job development.
- **Growth of the Tech Sector:** The creation of 5G services and applications promotes innovation and expansion in the tech sector. New applications, such as augmented reality (AR) and virtual reality (VR) experiences and Internet of Things (IoT) solutions, are being developed by startups and IT companies.

6.1.3. **Enhanced Digital Transformation and Connectivity**

The capabilities of 5G facilitate digital transformation in a number of industries:

- **Transportation:** 5G is necessary for connected and autonomous vehicles (CAVs) to communicate in real time with other cars and infrastructure. This improves fuel efficiency, lowers accident rates, and manages traffic better. At the forefront of this revolution are businesses like Tesla and Waymo, who are testing and implementing CAVs that make use of 5G connectivity.
- **Smart Cities:** 5G makes it possible to create networked systems for trash management, public safety, and energy management in smart cities. Barcelona, for example, uses real-time monitoring and emergency response systems to improve public safety, optimize traffic flow, and lower energy usage through the deployment of 5G technology.

6.1.4. **Support for Emerging Technologies**

5G lays the groundwork for developing technologies, opening up fresh business prospects:

- **IoT:** 5G greatly enhances the IoT ecosystem by enabling a large number of devices to connect with ease. Applications in logistics (real-time tracking), home automation (smart homes), and agricultural (smart farming) are made possible by this connectivity. To increase agricultural output, John Deere, for instance, employs 5G-connected sensors to improve crop yields and monitor soil health.
- **AR/VR:** 5G networks with high speeds make it easier for AR and VR apps to be widely adopted. Retailers such as IKEA are using augmented reality (AR) to improve the shopping experience and boost sales by allowing customers to see furniture in their homes before making a purchase.

6.1.5. **Worldwide Competitiveness**

Investing in 5G infrastructure gives nations an advantage over rivals in the international market:

- **Export Potential:** Countries in the forefront of 5G technology have the ability to export knowledge, gear, and services. As a leader in 5G rollout, South Korea has expanded its economy by becoming a significant exporter of 5G services and technology.
- **Attracting Investments:** Businesses aiming to profit from enhanced connectivity are drawn to foreign direct investment (FDI) produced by robust 5G infrastructure. For instance, as it works to establish itself as a

digital hub by expanding its 5G network, the UK has seen a rise in foreign direct investment in the tech industry.

In summary, the financial advantages of 5G are extensive and diverse. 5G is expected to be a driving force behind innovation and economic growth, with benefits such as increased productivity, job creation, and support for developing technologies and digital transformation. Its influence will be felt in all sectors of the economy, increasing productivity, improving communication, and putting countries in a competitive position internationally. The future of the global economy will be shaped by 5G networks as their full economic potential becomes more and more evident as they roll out.

6.2. Social Changes Driven by 5G

The introduction of 5G technology is causing significant societal shifts in addition to economic transformation. 5G's rapid speed, low latency, and wide-spread connectivity are expected to have an impact on a number of societal issues, including social interactions, urban development, healthcare, and education. Here are several significant societal shifts brought about by 5G, along with striking examples:

6.2.1. Improved Quality and Access to Healthcare

5G is transforming healthcare by raising the standard of treatment and facilitating better access to medical services:

- **Telemedicine:** 5G will enable telemedicine services to share real-time data and provide high-definition video consultations, which will improve the efficacy of remote diagnosis and treatment. For example, 5G-enabled telemedicine is enabling patients in rural India who would otherwise have to travel great distances for care to receive specialized consultations.
- **Remote Surgery:** With the aid of robotic technology managed over 5G networks, surgeons are able to carry out intricate treatments remotely. One remarkable instance is the first-ever remote brain surgery was out in China, in which a Beijing-based surgeon used a 5G network to successfully perform surgery on a patient who was 3,000 kilometers distant.

6.2.2. Revolutionizing Learning and Education

Immersion and interactive learning experiences are being made possible by 5G technology, which is changing education:

- **Virtual Classrooms:** 5G makes it possible to set up online learning environments where students from all over the world may take part in interactive, real-time classes. In order to improve the quality of education during the COVID-19 pandemic, South Korean schools made use of 5G networks to host virtual reality (VR) and live interactivity in online classes.
- **AR/VR:** With the help of 5G, augmented reality (AR) and virtual reality (VR) can be used to build immersive learning environments. For instance, Case Western Reserve University's medical students study human anatomy using 3D holograms via 5G-enabled AR and VR, which makes for a more effective and engaging learning environment than traditional teaching techniques.

6.2.3. Changing Social Exchanges and Interconnectedness

5G is changing how people communicate and engage with one another:

- **Improved Social Media Experiences**: Richer, more interactive experiences can be had on social media sites thanks to quicker data rates. Users can share HD films, stream live content, and instantly apply augmented reality filters. 5G is being used by platforms such as Instagram and TikTok to improve user engagement and content production.
- **Virtual Reality Social Spaces:** 5G makes it possible to establish online communities in which individuals can gather together, socialize, and participate in activities. Avatar creation and virtual environment socialization are made possible by platforms such as Facebook Horizon and VRChat, which are gaining popularity and removing geographical constraints.

6.2.4. Smart Cities and Higher Living Standards

A key component of smart city development, which aims to raise inhabitants' quality of life, is 5G:

- **Smart Infrastructure:** 5G enables the installation of smart lighting, waste management programs, and intelligent traffic management systems. Smart transportation and effective energy management are two ways that Singapore's Smart Nation plan leverages 5G to improve urban living.
- **Public Safety and Emergency Response:** By facilitating real-time monitoring and quicker emergency response, 5G enhances public safety. For instance, 5G-connected drones are utilized in the Netherlands for emergency response, giving first responders access to real-time video feeds that facilitate better situation assessment and management.

6.2.5. Overcoming the Digital Divide

5G has the ability to close the digital divide by giving underserved and distant places access to high-speed internet:

- **Rural Connectivity:** 5G is being used to give rural residents in various regions of Africa access to the internet in areas where traditional broadband infrastructure is inadequate. These communities can benefit from increased access to telehealth services, educational materials, and employment possibilities made possible by this link.
- **Cheap Internet:** 5G has the potential to increase market competition for internet services, which will lower prices and make high-speed internet more accessible. For example, the introduction of 5G is anticipated to lower data costs in nations like India, increasing the accessibility of internet services for a larger portion of the populace.

In summary, 5G is causing significant and varied social impacts. 5G is expected to improve people's quality of life through changing social interactions, improving healthcare, revolutionizing education, and fostering the growth of smart cities. Its ability to close the digital gap further guarantees that these advantages are shared more fairly, promoting increased social cohesiveness and inclusion. The impact of 5G technology on society will only increase as it develops and spreads, bringing us a new era of innovation and connectivity.

6.3. 5G and Global Connectivity

Compared to current 3G/4G networks, societies will be able to connect at substantially quicker speeds thanks to the fifth generation of cellular networks (5G). Additionally, *Machine-To-Machine* (M2M) communication is anticipated to be made possible by 5G, opening up new avenues for interconnectivity that might power the *Internet of Things* (IoT) and revolutionize a variety of industries.

Although the "Core" and "RAN" (or Edge) components of a network's architecture have historically been separated, the lines between these two categories are becoming increasingly blurred in 5G networks as the functions of the core are combined with those of the RAN. The deployment of 5G networks will also result in a significant rise in the quantity of supporting infrastructure needed. Additionally, many nations are eager to be among the first to adopt and deploy 5G due to the advantages it can provide in terms of connectivity and the economy.

Decision-makers now need to appropriately take into account a variety of policy considerations that have arisen from all of these worries. These policy discussions, which take place against the backdrop of great power competition, go beyond the well-known worries about network resilience and infrastructure integrity to address issues like obtaining strategic advantage and having an impact on global standards-setting.

Thus, the introduction of 5G technology, which promises previously unheard-of speeds, extremely low latency, and the ability to link a large number of devices at once, represents a significant turning point in the development of global connection. This development is going to change the way we interact, communicate, and do business internationally. These are some of the main sectors, supported by compelling examples, where 5G is accelerating global connectivity:

6.3.1. **Transforming Communication Networks:**
Global communication networks are improved by 5G, which makes them quicker and more dependable:
- **Real-Time Communication:** is made possible even across great distances by 5G's ultra-low latency support. For applications like online gaming and video conferencing, this is essential. Multinational corporations such as Microsoft and Google are utilizing 5G technology to offer smooth video conferencing services, hence enhancing international business cooperation.
- **Cross-National Cooperation**: Teams operating on separate continents can collaborate more successfully because to improved connection. Thanks to the dependable and fast connections offered by 5G, a design team in the US may work in real time with production teams in China.

6.3.2. **Encouraging Global Trade and Business**
5G enhances supply chain management and logistics to enable more effective international trade and commerce:
- **Smart Logistics:** 5G enables IoT devices to track and manage commodities in real-time, resulting in more transparent and efficient supply chains. Businesses like DHL are monitoring their global fleets and shipments with 5G-powered IoT solutions to cut down on losses and delays.
- **E-Commerce Expansion:** E-commerce platforms can reach a wider audience thanks to faster and more dependable mobile internet connection. 5G enables companies like Amazon and Alibaba to provide customers with

faster, more engaging shopping experiences, such as AR-based product try-ons and high-definition product films.

6.3.3. Enabling Internet of Things (IoT)

The Internet of Things is growing thanks to 5G, which is linking billions of devices worldwide:

- **Smart Cities:** Thanks to 5G-enabled IoT, cities all around the world are becoming smarter. Barcelona, for instance, connects waste management, traffic signal, and streetlight systems over 5G, maximizing energy efficiency and enhancing public services.
- **Agriculture:** By linking gadgets like drones, self-driving tractors, and soil sensors, 5G is revolutionizing the agricultural industry. Farmers in the Netherlands are using 5G to track crop health and soil conditions in real time, which boosts sustainability and productivity.

6.3.4. Progressing Worldwide in Healthcare

5G is expected to transform healthcare by enabling worldwide access to cutting-edge medical services:

- **Telehealth and Remote Diagnostics:** 5G makes real-time data exchange and high-quality video consultations possible, opening up access to healthcare for underserved and remote places. For example, 5G is being used by telehealth providers in Africa to offer patients in remote areas specialized consultations.
- **Remote Surgery:** With 5G technology, surgeons may operate from a distance. One of the first instances of this is a remote surgery carried out in China, when a surgeon in Beijing used a 5G network to operate successfully on a patient from thousands of kilometers away. This shows how specialized care may be provided anywhere in the world.

6.3.5. Encouraging International Research and Education

5G makes education and research more transformative by enabling improved connectivity and resource access:

- **Virtual Classrooms:** 5G makes it possible for students to learn together from around the globe in virtual classrooms that provide immersive, interactive learning opportunities. For example, academic institutions such as Harvard and MIT are investigating the potential of 5G to develop worldwide virtual and augmented reality learning systems.

- **Collaborative Research:** Regardless of their location, researchers can share huge datasets and work together in real-time on projects. 5G is being used by the European Organization for Nuclear Research (CERN) to improve its data-sharing capabilities, allowing experts to work together on high-energy physics research from all around the world.

6.3.6. Fostering Inclusive Growth and Closing the Digital Divide

5G has the ability to encourage economic inclusion and close the digital gap:

- **Rural and Distant Connectivity:** Previously underserved rural and distant locations can now enjoy high-speed internet connectivity thanks to 5G. 5G is being implemented in nations such as India in order to improve education, healthcare, and economic prospects by providing internet connectivity to remote regions.

- **Affordably priced Internet Access:** 5G's enhanced efficiency and competition may lower the price of internet access. For instance, a greater percentage of the populace now enjoys cheaper and easier access to high-speed internet thanks to South Korea's extensive 5G infrastructure.

In summary, the revolutionary 5G technology greatly improves worldwide connectivity. 5G is expected to make the globe more open and interconnected by transforming communication networks, fostering international trade, allowing IoT, improving healthcare, assisting with global education, and promoting economic inclusion. 5G's influence on global connectivity will only grow as it spreads and develops, creating new opportunities and bridging gaps across many industries and geographical areas.

Chapter 7: Challenges and Solutions in 5G Deployment

7.1. Technical Challenges

In the rapidly evolving field of technology, 5G is the newest big thing. It's similar to the rock star who claims to be able to connect anything from your car to your fridge and offer reduced latency and quicker speeds. But like any celebrity, 5G has its share of behind-the-scenes issues. Many technical issues related to the deployment of 5G technology must be resolved in order to guarantee its effective installation and functioning. This chapter explores the main technical issues surrounding the deployment of 5G and, where appropriate, offers examples and possible solutions.

7.1.1. Spectrum Availability and Management Challenge:

- **Challenge:** For 5G networks, spectrum availability and management are essential. For 5G to fully realize its potential, a combination of low-, mid-, and high-frequency bands is needed. However, the distribution of spectrum among various nations and areas is frequently uneven and fragmented.
- **Example:** The Federal Communications Commission (FCC) of the United States has allotted many frequency bands for 5G, including as the millimeter-wave (mmWave), 3.5 GHz, and 600 MHz bands. But the mid-band spectrum, which strikes a compromise between capacity and coverage, is scarce and fiercely disputed.
- **Solution:** Governments and regulatory organizations must standardize spectrum distribution worldwide in order to address spectrum-related issues. Spectrum shortage can also be lessened by using dynamic spectrum sharing (DSS) technology, which enables operators to use current 4G LTE spectrum for 5G. Furthermore, with enhanced beamforming and small cell deployment, the usage of mmWave bands can be optimized despite their limited penetration and range.

7.1.2. Infrastructure Requirements

- **Challenge:** To attain high speeds and low latency, 5G networks need a dense infrastructure of fiber optics, base stations, and tiny cells. This infrastructure can be expensive and hard to deploy, particularly in metropolitan areas.

- **Example:** To support 5G mmWave technology, tiny cell deployment is required in cities like New York and San Francisco. But getting through governmental permissions, finding appropriate sites, and resolving neighborhood aesthetic objections are all part of the process.
- **Solution:** The deployment process can be streamlined by creating public-private partnerships, mounting tiny cells on existing infrastructure (such as utility poles and streetlights), and utilizing cutting-edge technologies like drone-assisted inspections and installs. Furthermore, utilizing network function virtualization (NFV) and software-defined networking (SDN) can aid in building more adaptable and scalable networks.

7.1.3. Energy Consumption Challenge:

- **Challenge:** Larger data volumes and more connected devices are anticipated for 5G networks, which would result in higher energy consumption. Concerns are raised over the impact on the environment and operational costs.
- **Example**: according to a Huawei study, a single 5G base station may use up to three times as much energy as a single 4G base station. When several base stations are needed in highly populated areas, this becomes especially difficult.
- **Solution:** Network operators can use energy-efficient technology like massive MIMO (Multiple Input Multiple Output), which increases spectral efficiency, to reduce energy consumption. Investing in renewable energy sources and smart grid technology, together with using AI and machine learning algorithms to optimize network performance and energy utilization, can all help lower the carbon footprint.

7.1.4. Security and Privacy Challenge:

- **Challenge:** There are serious security and privacy issues associated with 5G's expanded capabilities, which include enhanced connection and IoT integration. Cyberattacks, data breaches, and illegal access to vital infrastructure are examples of potential risks.
- **Example:** greater IoT device utilization in 5G networks may lead to greater opportunities for cyberattacks to enter the system. The 2016 Mirai botnet assault exposed the possible weaknesses in a highly networked 5G environment by using IoT devices to conduct a huge DDoS attack.

- **Solution:** Reducing security threats can be accomplished by strengthening security measures such robust authentication protocols, end-to-end encryption, and network slicing, which makes it possible to create isolated virtual networks. Stakeholder sharing of threat intelligence, regular security audits, and the enforcement of strict data protection laws are also essential.

7.1.5. Signal Propagation Challenge and Interference:

- **Challenge:** 5G's high-frequency signals, particularly those in the mmWave bands, are susceptible to interference and have a restricted range and penetration via foliage and structures.
- **Example:** In metropolitan settings, mmWave transmissions can be severely hindered by buildings and other structures, which can cause uneven coverage and connectivity problems.
- **Solution:** You can improve signal strength and coverage by deploying a dense network of tiny cells and utilizing cutting-edge technology like massive MIMO and beamforming. Furthermore, combining mmWave with low- and mid-band frequencies can result in a 5G network that is more stable and balanced.

7.1.6. Device Compatibility and User Adoption Difficulty:

- **Challenge:** The switch to 5G necessitates suitable devices, and because of their price and availability, securing mass adoption can be difficult.
- **Example:** the first 5G cellphones and gadgets were pricy and had a little selection. The adoption of 5G services by users and their entire rollout may be slowed back by this initial obstacle.
- **Solution:** It is anticipated that the price of 5G-compatible devices will drop as the technology advances. User adoption can also be accelerated by providing subsidies or incentives to manufacturers in order to encourage them to provide a greater choice of reasonably priced 5G devices. Furthermore, 4G networks' backward compatibility guarantees a seamless transition for users with no connectivity problems.

In summary, to fully exploit the potential of 5G technology, a number of technical problems related to its deployment must be resolved. Stakeholders can guarantee the effective deployment of 5G networks by addressing difficulties with spectrum management, infrastructure needs, energy consumption, security, interference, and device compatibility. By use of cooperative endeavors and inventive resolutions, the revolutionary advantages of 5G can be utilized to propel worldwide connectedness and technological progress.

The implementation of 5G technology necessitates negotiating a challenging terrain of laws and regulations. The speed and effectiveness of 5G rollouts may be greatly impacted by these issues, which may affect how soon society can take use of this game-changing technology. This chapter explores the main legal and policy issues surrounding the rollout of 5G, including relevant instances and possible fixes.

7.2.1. Spectrum Allocation and Licensing

- **Challenge:** The successful deployment of 5G depends on efficient spectrum allocation and licensing. Unfortunately, there may be delays and irregularities in availability due to the drawn-out and politically charged nature of the procedure.
- **Example:** different nations allocate spectrum in different ways. The Federal Communications Commission (FCC) in the US auctions out frequency bands to the highest bidders, which can cause delays and exorbitant expenses. Certain European nations, on the other hand, have taken a more cooperative stance when it comes to spectrum allocation, using either direct assignment or regional sharing agreements.
- **Solution:** Regulatory agencies should use more adaptable and dynamic licensing schemes to simplify the distribution of spectrum. To guarantee more effective use, for example, unlicensed spectrum uses and spectrum sharing can be encouraged. International cooperation and harmonization of spectrum policies can also be beneficial in reducing inter-country interference and guaranteeing uninterrupted worldwide connection.

7.2.2. Infrastructure Deployment Regulations:

- **Challenge:** One major obstacle to the widespread adoption of 5G technology could be the legislative framework for infrastructure deployment. Community opposition, environmental constraints, and local zoning laws can all make it difficult to deploy base stations and small cells—two pieces of essential infrastructure.
- **Example:** Telecommunication companies in the UK have had difficulties implementing 5G infrastructure as a result of strict local authority approval

procedures and planning requirements. The rollout of 5G has been delayed down by these obstacles, especially in urban areas where dense networks are most needed.

- **Solution:** Governments can simplify rules and offer precise directives for the installation of 5G infrastructure. In order to accelerate infrastructure development, this can involve lowering bureaucratic red tape, putting in place standardized approval procedures, and encouraging public-private collaborations. Early planning phase engagement with stakeholders and local communities can also help allay fears and increase support for 5G initiatives.

7.2.3. Safety and Health Issues

- **Challenge:** Opposition and regulatory obstacles may arise from public worries about the health and safety consequences of 5G technology, particularly with relation to radiation exposure.
- **Example:** As residents voiced worries about possible health problems linked with RF radiation, public protests and petitions in Switzerland caused delays in the rollout of 5G. The Swiss government has responded to this by launching a thorough investigation and enforcing more stringent guidelines on 5G deployments.
- **Solution:** Research based on evidence and open communication are necessary to address health and safety issues. Scientific research evaluating the health effects of radiofrequency radiation ought to be funded and shared by governments and regulatory organizations. Campaigns for public education that provide precise and lucid information regarding the safety of 5G technology can also assist allay worries.

7.2.4. Cybersecurity and Privacy Regulations:

- **Challenges:** Significant cybersecurity and privacy risks are raised by 5G networks' increasing connectivity and data transfer capabilities. It is crucial to have strong regulatory frameworks in place to defend consumer data and prevent cyberattacks.
- **Example:** To safeguard user data privacy, the European Union enacted the General Data Protection Regulation (GDPR). However, the introduction of 5G brings with it additional difficulties, like the safe management of enormous volumes of data across national borders and the integration of IoT devices.

- **Solution:** It's imperative to update current privacy laws and create thorough cybersecurity standards. This entails putting in place network slicing for security isolation, requiring robust encryption, and imposing strict data protection regulations. In order to combat cross-border cybersecurity risks and create global 5G standards, international cooperation is also essential.

7.2.5. Standardization and compatibility

- **Challenge:** The smooth operation and widespread adoption of 5G technology may be hampered by the absence of established protocols and compatibility between various 5G networks and devices.
- **Example:** Because different telecom operators and equipment manufacturers use different standards and technologies, early 5G deployments have shown inconsistent network performance and device compatibility.
- **Solution:** The development and harmonization of 5G standards is greatly aided by international standardization organizations like the Third Generation Partnership Project (3GPP) and the International Telecommunication Union (ITU). Encouraging cooperation between industry participants, such as regulators, equipment makers, and telecom operators, helps guarantee that standards are broadly accepted and put into practice. This will make interoperability easier and offer a unified user experience among various networks and geographical areas.

7.2.6. Digital Divide and Accessibility

- **Challenge:** There are a lot of legislative and policy issues to resolve before 5G technology can be widely used. If 5G is implemented without taking the necessary precautions, the digital divide may widen and impoverished and rural areas would be severely disadvantaged.
- **Example:** urban areas in the US are more likely than rural ones to get 5G service sooner. In rural areas, the financial case for investment is weaker because of lower population densities and greater deployment costs.
- **Solution:** The deployment of 5G in underserved and rural areas can be encouraged by the implementation of laws and incentives by governments. This can include tax breaks, grants, or subsidies for telecom companies who make investments in certain areas. Partnerships with commercial businesses and public funding initiatives can also aid in closing the digital gap and guaranteeing that all communities can take use of 5G's advantages.

In summary, navigating a wide range of complicated regulatory and policy obstacles is necessary for the deployment of 5G technology. Stakeholders can assist in the effective rollout of 5G networks by resolving concerns with spectrum allocation, infrastructure development, cybersecurity, standardization, and accessibility. The revolutionary potential of 5G can be used to propel worldwide connection and technological improvement while making sure that its advantages are fairly dispersed across all societal segments through cooperative efforts and proactive regulatory frameworks.

7.3. Addressing Security Concerns

The implementation of 5G technology raises a number of security issues that need to be resolved in order to shield people, devices, and networks from possible dangers. The stakes are higher than ever with 5G networks supporting a huge number of connected devices and essential services. This chapter addresses the main security issues surrounding the introduction of 5G, gives instances of these difficulties, and suggests ways to address them.

7.3.1. **Increasing Attack Surface**

- **Challenge:** 5G networks' enhanced connectivity and IoT integration raise the possibility of cyberattack entry sites. Ensuring the security of billions of linked devices becomes a major concern.
- **Example:** the 2016 Mirai botnet attack launched a massive distributed denial-of-service (DDoS) attack by taking use of flaws in Internet of Things devices. As 5G links even more devices, the possibility of such attacks increases.
- **Solution:** It's critical to have strong security standards for Internet of Things devices. This includes regular firmware upgrades, required security certifications for Internet of Things devices, and default security settings that demand encryption and strong passwords. Furthermore, by isolating vulnerable devices, network segmentation and micro-segmentation can lessen the impact of an attack.

7.3.2. **Network Slicing Security:**

- **Challenge:** Network slicing makes it possible for several virtual networks to function on a single physical infrastructure. Although each slice can be customized for a particular application, this poses new security risks because a breach in one slice may have an effect on others.

- **Example:** Utilities, emergency services, and public transit may each use an own network slice in a smart city. If not appropriately isolated, a security breach in the public transportation slice may have an impact on the emergency services slice.
- **Solution:** It is imperative to maintain robust isolation between network slices. Secure network slicing architectures that impose stringent access rules and separation can help achieve this. Network slices can be made more flexible and secure by utilizing technologies like network function virtualization (NFV) and software-defined networking (SDN). Every slice can benefit from routine security audits and monitoring, which can quickly identify and neutralize threats.

7.3.3. Supply Chain Security:

- **Challenge:** 5G infrastructure comprises a large number of parts from different vendors, which raises questions regarding supply chain security. Vulnerabilities may be introduced at any point in the supply chain by malicious actors.
- **Example:** worries have been expressed over the usage of equipment from specific vendors, like Huawei, in 5G networks because of possible connections to foreign governments and the possibility of sabotage or espionage.
- **Solution:** It's crucial to put in place a stringent supplier and equipment certification and vetting procedure. Best practices for supply chain risk management, such as utilizing diversified supply chains to lessen reliance on any one provider, procuring from reliable suppliers, and performing frequent security assessments, should be used by governments and telecom operators. Creating a transparent and safe supply chain helps reduce the dangers brought on by rogue elements.

7.3.4. Data Privacy and Protection

- **Challenge:** There are a lot of data privacy and protection issues with 5G networks because of their higher data throughput and variety of applications. It is necessary to protect sensitive data sent over 5G networks against breaches and illegal access.
- **Example:** stringent privacy measures are necessary for healthcare apps that use 5G to transfer patient data for telemedicine and remote monitoring in

order to comply with US laws like the Health Insurance Portability and Accountability Act (HIPAA).

- **Solution:** To safeguard sensitive data, end-to-end encryption must be used for both data in transit and data at rest. Technologies that improve privacy, such secure multi-party computation, anonymization, and Pseudonymization, can further protect user data. Maintaining privacy is ensured by adherence to data protection laws, such as the General Data Protection Regulation (GDPR) in Europe. Frequent security training for stakeholders and staff can also aid in preventing human error-related data breaches.

7.3.5. Threat Detection and Response

- **Challenge:** 5G networks' complexity and size make threat detection and response more difficult. It's possible that conventional security measures won't be enough to quickly identify and neutralize sophisticated attackers.
- **Example:** advanced persistent threats (APTs) have the ability to enter networks, stay hidden for a long time, collect sensitive data, and do a great deal of harm.
- **Solution:** Threat detection and response skills can be improved by utilizing machine learning (ML) and artificial intelligence (AI). Security systems powered by AI are able to instantly identify risks, analyze trends in network traffic, and spot irregularities. Centralized monitoring and analysis of security events is made possible by the implementation of a strong Security Information and Event Management (SIEM) system. Regular vulnerability assessments and penetration tests can also be used to find and fix possible security holes.

7.3.6. Challenges with Regulation and Compliance

- **Problem:** One of the biggest obstacles to the deployment of 5G is ensuring compliance with several national and international security legislation and standards. It is challenging to apply a single security strategy across different regions due to their disparate needs.
- **Example:** the GDPR of the European Union mandates stringent data protection procedures, yet the US has distinct laws governing cybersecurity and data privacy. In order to assure compliance, telecom operators developing 5G networks worldwide need to traverse these regulatory environments.

- **Solution**: It's crucial to create a thorough compliance plan that complies with the strictest security guidelines in every area. To prove compliance with pertinent regulations, this entails routine audits, documentation, and reporting. Ongoing compliance can be ensured by working together with regulatory organizations to stay informed about changing standards and best practices. Implementing global security guidelines, like ISO/IEC 27001, can offer a strong basis for following regulations.

In summary, *in order to fully utilize this revolutionary technology, 5G deployment security issues must be resolved*. Stakeholders may construct robust and secure 5G networks by addressing issues with the expanded attack surface, network slicing, supply chain security, data privacy, threat detection, and regulatory compliance. The security threats related to 5G can be reduced by combining cutting-edge technologies, strong security standards, and preventative actions, guaranteeing a dependable and secure digital future.

Chapter 8: Looking Beyond 5G: The Path to 6G

8.1. 6G: What exactly is it?

6G stands for *Sixth Generation Mobile Connectivity*, as the name would imply. Although the final shape of 6G remains unknown until it is standardized, it is not too soon to make assumptions about the technology it will contain and the features it will possess. It's clear that the backend modifications done to mobile networks to support 5G will help 5G.

In order to improve signal quality, particularly indoors, operators have densified radio networks by adding more antennas. Additionally, edge computing and cloud technologies allow data to be handled closer to consumers, even at the mast level, resulting in significantly reduced latency.

In comparison to 5G networks, 6G networks will be able to use higher frequencies while offering significantly more capacity and significantly lower latency. Supporting communications with a latency of one microsecond is one of the objectives of the 6G internet. This is 1,000 times faster than a millisecond throughput, or 1/1000th of the delay. The market for 6G technology is anticipated to enable significant advancements in the fields of imaging, location awareness, and presence technologies. The 6G computational infrastructure will be able to determine the optimal location for computing, including choices about data processing, sharing, and storage, in concert with artificial intelligence (AI).

It is crucial to remember that 6G is not an operational technology just yet. The industry standards for 6G-enabled network equipment are still years away, despite the fact that certain vendors are investing in the next generation wireless standard.

8.2. How 6G Differs from 5G?

The speed difference is the most noticeable. In comparison to 5G, 6G will make use of more sophisticated radio equipment as well as a larger volume and diversity of airwaves, including Extreme High Frequency (EHF) spectrum, which allows for extremely high speeds and massive capacity across short distances.

6G will theoretically offer terabit speeds, whereas 5G will break the gigabit barrier and 4G speeds were discussed in terms of megabits. Although the majority of customers will receive more than 100Gbps, this bitrate is still transformative. 6G has the potential to cover everything. Intelligent surfaces that can reflect electromagnetic signals and 6G satellite technology will bring multi-gigabit connection with low latency to regions of the world that have been too costly or difficult to access with traditional mobile networks.

The skies, the oceans, and remote regions of the world may all be interconnected. Although 5G utilizes artificial intelligence (AI) for data processing, dynamic resource allocation, and optimization, 6G will be able to give ubiquitous, integrated intelligence due to its distributed architecture and extremely low latency of less than one millisecond. In fact, according to Japanese operator NTT DoCoMo, 6G would enable artificial intelligence (AI) akin to that of the human brain. In addition, 6G will use less electricity and be more efficient than its predecessor. A more sustainable mobile industry depends on energy efficiency due to the projected increase in data generation.

8.3. How 6G will Operate

Increased throughput, increased capacity, and decreased latency will enable more devices to be connected to the network, remove the limitations of local processing power for applications, and obfuscate the distinction between the digital, human, and physical worlds. While current services will change, 6G might be the network that brings use cases out of science fiction at last. Terabit speeds will undoubtedly improve the Netflix experience and make FaceTime calls less uncomfortable, but more connected "things" and widespread coverage will alter how we interact with technology and perhaps even the globe.

Digital services that are aware of location and context will be made possible by 6G, along with immersive experiences like high-fidelity holograms and completely immersive extended reality (XR). With wearable sensors, real-time VR communication will be available in place of Zoom calls, giving users the impression that they are physically in the same room. The Internet of Things (IoT) will grow and develop, giving apps access to more data and greater power.

While the expansion of 6G coverage to the sky and oceans could help linked maritime, aviation, and possibly space applications, real-time AI has the potential to revolutionize robotics. Furthermore, since 6G uses so much less energy than 5G, it might even be able to charge low-power Internet of Things devices through the network, which would change the economics of large-scale deployments and promote sustainability.

8.4. Capability of 6G Network

It is anticipated that different frequencies would be used selectively by 6G wireless sensing systems in order to evaluate absorption and modify frequencies correspondingly. Because electromagnetic radiation is emitted and absorbed at distinct frequencies by atoms and molecules, and because these frequencies are constant for any given substance, this method is made possible.

Many government and industry approaches to public safety and critical asset protection will be significantly impacted by 6G, including the following:

- Health monitoring,
- Air quality measurements,
- Threat detection,
- Gas and toxicity sensing,
- Real-life-like sensory interfaces
- Feature and facial recognition,
- Decision-making in fields like law enforcement and social credit systems.

Advancements in these domains will also have a positive impact on developing technologies like Virtual reality, Augmented reality, Smart cities, and Driverless cars, as well as smartphones and other mobile network technologies.

8.5. Who's Behind 6G Development?

Considering the emergence of mobile connectivity as a front in geopolitical conflicts, it is hardly surprising that governments everywhere want to be at the forefront of the developing field of 6G technology.

Many industry players are paying attention to the race to 6G. Keysight Technologies, a test and measurement manufacturer, has pledged to support its advancement. Leading infrastructure firms, including Samsung, Nokia, and Huawei, have hinted that they are working on 6G research and development.

When compared to the struggle to determine which businesses and nations would rule the 6G market and its associated applications and services, the race to achieve 5G may prove to be insignificant. Among the significant initiatives in progress are the following:

- **China's Ministry of Industry and Information Technology** is funding and overseeing national 6G research and development.
- **U.S. Federal Communications Commission (FCC)**: In 2020, the U.S. Federal Communications Commission (FCC) made the 6G frequency available for spectrum testing, covering frequencies from 3 THz to 95 GHz.
- **Adelaide University in Australia and Osaka University in Japan**: Researchers from Adelaide University in Australia and Osaka University in Japan have created a silicon-based microprocessor with a unique multiplex to split data and allow for more effective management of terahertz radiation. Researchers stated that during testing, the device sent data at a rate of 11 gigabits per second, which is higher than the 10 Gbps theoretical limit of 5G.
- **Electronics and Telecommunications Research Institute in South Korea**: Research in the terahertz frequency band for 6G is being done at the Electronics and Telecommunications Research Institute in South Korea. It predicts data speeds that are five times faster than 5G networks and 100 times faster than 4G Long-Term Evolution (LTE) networks.
- **University of Oulu in Finland:** To create a 6G vision for 2030, the University of Oulu in Finland has started the 6Genesis research project. In addition, the university and Japan's Beyond 5G Promotion Consortium have inked a cooperation agreement to manage the Finnish 6G Flagship research team's 6G efforts.
- **Hexa-X**: A European consortium of leading figures from academia and business that is advancing research on 6G standards. Leading that project is the Finnish communications corporation Nokia; other participants are the Swedish operator Ericsson and the Italian operator TIM.

8.6. Early Research and Development in 6G

The advancement of wireless communication is still ongoing, as experts in the field and academia begin to concentrate on the upcoming 6G technology. While 5G deployment is still continuing strong globally, *6G research attempts to solve 5G's shortcomings and open up previously unthinkable new applications and services.*

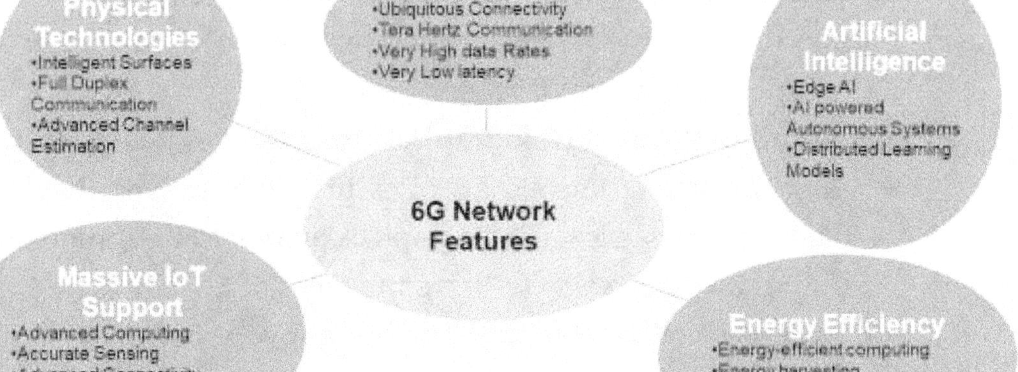

Source: "The Future of Connectivity: Unleashing the Power of 5G and Beyond", GoodMan Series, (Patrick Mukosha, 2024)

Figure 9: 5G Network Features

8.6.1. Key Topics in 6G Research and Development:

8.6.1.1. Terahertz (THz) Frequencies

- **Concept:** Compared to 5G's millimeter-wave frequencies, which offer much less bandwidth, 6G seeks to utilize the THz frequency spectrum (0.1–10 THz), which offers substantially more capacity.

- **Example:** Ultra-high-speed wireless communication using THz frequencies is possible, with a potential peak speed of 1 Tbps (terabits per second). For example, one might download an HD movie in its entirety.

- **Challenges:** In order to enable efficient THz communication, new materials and antenna technologies are needed due to high propagation loss and penetration concerns caused by the short wavelength of THz waves.

8.6.1.2. Sophisticated Machine Learning and Artificial Intelligence

- **Concept:** Combining cutting-edge AI and machine learning algorithms to maximize resource allocation, network performance, and adaptable communication techniques.
- **Example:** AI-driven fault management and predictive maintenance can improve network dependability by identifying and resolving problems before they have an impact on service.
- **Challenge:** Creating AI models that can manage the size and complexity of 6G networks while maintaining real-time performance and decision-making abilities is a challenge.

8.6.1.3. Communication through Holography and Extended Reality (XR):

- **Concept:** Immersion technologies that demand very low latency and high data rates, such as holographic communication, augmented reality (AR), and virtual reality (VR), are the focus of 6G.
- **Example:** holographic calls could improve social contact and remote collaboration by enabling users to engage in real-time engagement with 3D projections of other individuals.
- **Challenges** include creating compression methods to manage the enormous volumes of data involved and delivering the required data speeds and latency.

8.6.2. Virtualization and Network Slicing:

- **Concept:** Expanding upon 5G's network slicing capabilities, 6G seeks to provide more dynamic and granular slicing, allowing tailored virtual networks for various services and applications.
- **Example:** whereas smart homes might demand a slice tailored for cost-effectiveness and connectivity, autonomous cars require a dedicated network slice with assured low latency and high reliability.
- **Difficulties:** Keeping several network slices secure and isolated from one another while managing and coordinating them in real time.

8.6.3. Quantum Communication in Quantum:

- **Concept:** Using quantum technologies—like quantum key distribution (QKD) for unbreakable encryption—to improve security and open up new channels of communication.
- **Example:** consider using QKD to protect the transmission of sensitive data in official and financial communications.

- **Challenge:** The challenge lies in creating scalable and useful quantum communication systems that can be seamlessly integrated with conventional networks.

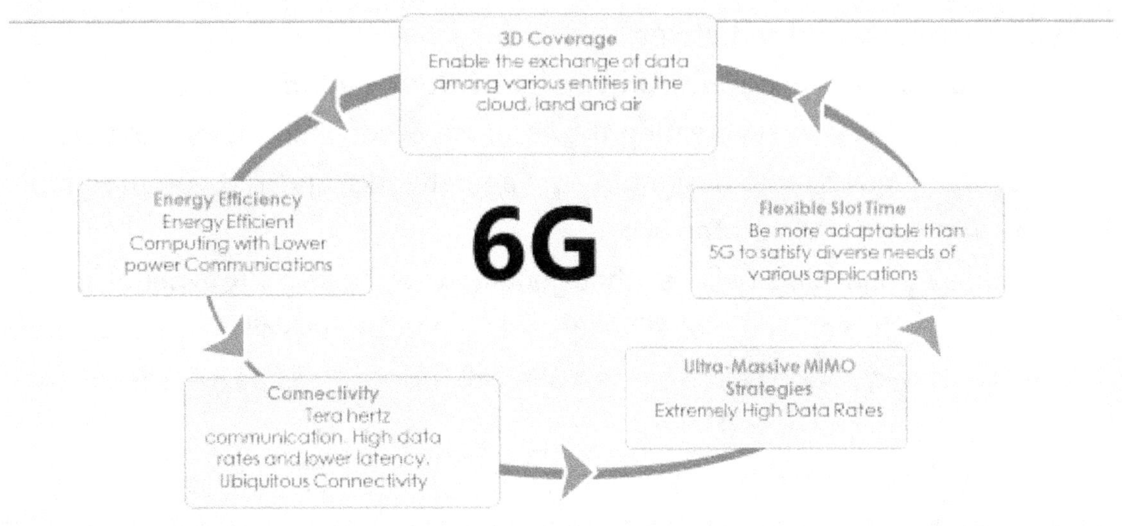

Source: "The Future of Connectivity: Unleashing the Power of 5G and Beyond", GoodMan Series, (Patrick Mukosha, 2024)

Figure 10: 6G Communication

8.6.4. Sustainable and Energy-Efficient Networks:

- **Concept:** Creating 6G networks with an emphasis on environmental impact reduction, energy conservation, and sustainability.
- **Example:** consider using renewable energy sources to power network infrastructure and putting energy-efficient protocols into place.
- **Challenges** include creating technology that facilitate green networking and striking a balance between the requirement to use less energy and achieve higher performance.

8.6.5. Important Players and Joint Ventures

Governmental organizations, business titans, and academic institutions are all driving 6G research and development. Important participants consist of:

- **Academic Institutions:** Leading universities in 6G research include the University of Oulu in Finland, home of the 6G Flagship program.

- **Leaders in the Industry:** Businesses substantially investing in 6G research, development, and standard-setting include Samsung, Nokia, Huawei, and Ericsson.
- **Government and Regulatory Organizations:** The International Telecommunication Union (ITU) and other international organizations are beginning to lay out the framework and spectrum distribution for 6G.

8.6.6. Typical Projects and Initiatives:

a. **6G Flagship Program (University of Oulu, Finland):**
- Focuses on creating the essential 6G enabling technologies, such as novel radio designs, AI-driven networks, and THz communication.

b. **Samsung's Vision for 6G:**
- Samsung believes that genuinely immersive XR experiences, digital copies, and high-fidelity mobile holograms will all be made possible by 6G. Their goal is to reach up to 1 Tbps of speed and 100 microsecond latency.

c. **Project Hexa-X (European Union):**
- Focuses on important research topics such intelligent connection, sustainability, and huge twinning in an effort to build the foundation for 6G.

8.6.7. 6G Experience:

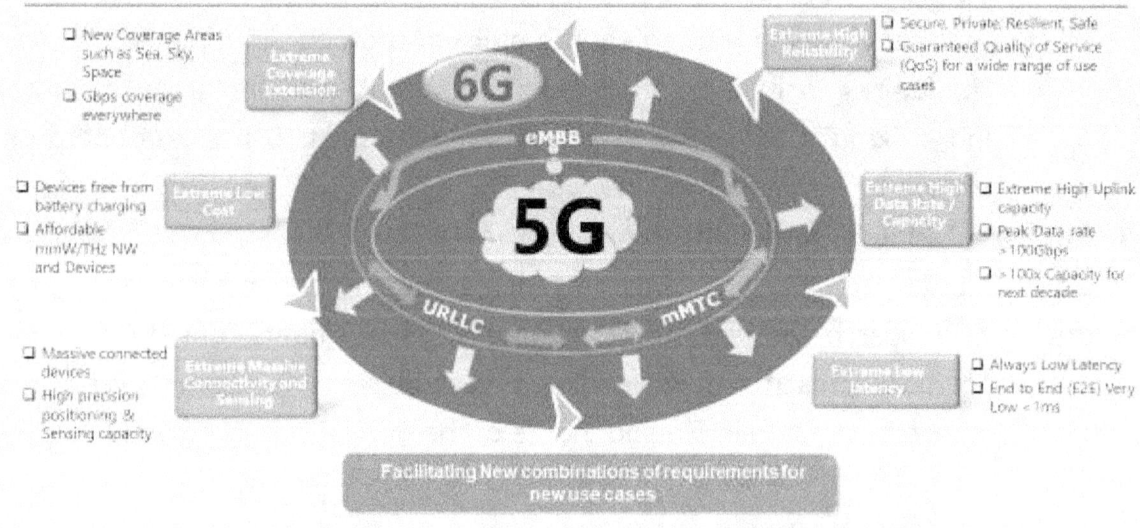

Source: "The Future of Connectivity: Unleashing the Power of 5G and Beyond", GoodMan Series, (Patrick Mukosha, 2024)

In summary, the next big advancement in wireless communication, *6G research and development addresses 5G's shortcomings and opens up possibilities for future uses*. The world's governments, businesses, and academic institutions are working together to provide the foundation for the 6G era, even though there are still many obstacles to overcome. These technologies will change how we interact, communicate, and perceive the digital world as they develop.

8.7. Addressing Security Concerns

The implementation of 5G technology raises a number of security issues that need to be resolved in order to shield people, devices, and networks from possible dangers. *The stakes are higher than ever with 5G networks supporting a huge number of connected devices and essential services.* This chapter addresses the main security issues surrounding the introduction of 5G, gives instances of these difficulties, and suggests ways to address them.

8.7.1. **Increasing Attack Surface**

a. Holographic Telepresence and Communication:

    I. **Concept:** With the help of 6G technology, holographic communication in real time would be possible, offering realistic 3D projections of people and objects.

    II. **Example:** picture attending a business conference where coworkers from all over the world appear as holograms, enabling natural gestures, eye contact, and spatial awareness just like they would if they were in person. This can have a substantial influence on both personal and corporate relationships by improving remote collaboration and lowering the need for travel.

    III. **Impact:** Holographic telepresence has the potential to transform a number of industries, including healthcare and education. In the former, teachers might work with specialists in other places to deliver immersive lectures to students around the world, while in the latter, doctors could consult with patients directly.

b. Advanced Healthcare and Telemedicine

    I. **Concept:** 6G will enable real-time patient monitoring with improved precision and dependability, remote surgery, and high-resolution medical imaging.

    II. **Example:** a surgeon in New York may use robotic tools controlled by a 6G network to carry out a difficult treatment on a patient in Tokyo. The robotic tools precisely and instantly reflect the actions of the surgeon because to 6G's extremely low latency and great dependability.

    III. **Impact:** By enabling access to specialist medical procedures in underserved or rural places, this skill can improve healthcare outcomes and lessen inequities. Furthermore, 6G-connected wearables with continuous remote monitoring can improve the management of chronic illnesses by warning medical professionals of possible problems before they get out of hand.

c. Autonomous Vehicles and Smart Transportation

    I. **Concept:** With improved vehicle-to-everything (V2X) connection made possible by 6G, autonomous transportation systems will be safer and more effective.

    II. **Example:** real-time communication between autonomous vehicles and traffic infrastructure will enable them to plan their movements, avert collisions, and maximize traffic flow. To ease traffic and increase safety, traffic lights in a smart city might, for example, dynamically change their settings in response to the presence of cars, pedestrians, and bicyclists.

    III. **Impact:** The extensive use of 6G-powered autonomous vehicles has the potential to significantly reduce traffic accidents, minimize emissions from better driving habits, and enhance mobility for those who are unable to operate a vehicle.

d. Immersive Extended Reality (XR)

    I. **Concept:** The bandwidth and latency required for genuinely immersive mixed reality (MR), virtual reality (VR), and augmented reality (AR) experiences will be supplied by 6G.

    II. **Example:** consumers might enjoy virtual concerts where they experience the sensation of being in the same room as the artists and other guests, mingling in real time. In the classroom, students may study intricate scientific ideas or historical events in a completely immersive setting, which would improve their comprehension and interest.

III. **Impact:** By offering new opportunities for learning, work, and play, these immersive experiences have the potential to revolutionize a variety of sectors, including real estate, education, entertainment, and training. Architects could utilize virtual reality (XR) to take clients through virtual models of structures prior to the start of construction.

e. **Smart Cities and IoT Integration:**

   I. **Concept:** With the help of 6G, billions of Internet of Things (IoT) devices will be able to be seamlessly integrated, resulting in more intelligent and responsive urban settings.

   II. **Example:** a smart city powered by 6G may have integrated waste management, transportation, energy management, and public safety systems. City planners and citizens might receive real-time data from sensors monitoring traffic, noise levels, and air quality around the city. By optimizing energy distribution according to demand, smart grids could cut expenses and waste.

   III. **Impact:** These developments may result in more efficient and sustainable cities, improving the standard of living for locals. Resource management, transportation congestion, and pollution are just a few of the urban issues that can be addressed with better data gathering and analysis.

f. **Automation in Industry and Automation 4.0**

   I. **Concept:** 6G will facilitate the next stage of industrial automation by providing extremely dependable, low-latency connection that will allow for real-time control systems, AI-driven operations, and sophisticated robotics.

   II. **Example:** in a factory equipped with 6G technology, machinery and robots might instantly communicate and coordinate their operations to maximize production lines and minimize downtime. Real-time sensor data analysis by AI algorithms could forecast equipment faults and initiate preventive maintenance.

   III. **Impact:** This could result in enhanced manufacturing flexibility, reduced production costs, and higher efficiency. Businesses can increase overall efficiency, adapt more swiftly to changes in the market, and customize products as needed.

g. **Global connection and Digital Inclusion**

I. **Concept:** The goal of 6G is to offer high-speed, universal connection, closing the gap between rich and poor people and guaranteeing that even the most remote and underprivileged places have access to the internet.

II. **Example:** satellite-based 6G networks or high-altitude platform stations (HAPS) may connect inaccessible islands, rural areas, and areas affected by disasters, guaranteeing constant communication and access to vital services.

III. **Impact:** 6G has the potential to enhance social inclusion, advance healthcare and education, and boost economic growth by democratizing access to ICTs. Additionally, improved communication can help with disaster recovery and emergency response.

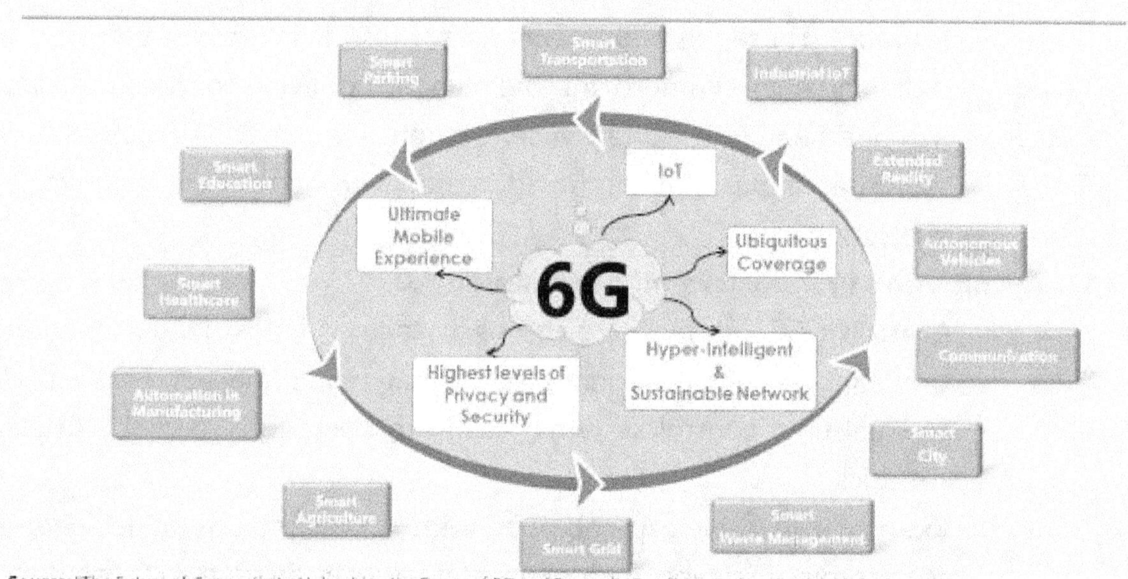

Source: "The Future of Connectivity: Unleashing the Power of 5G and Beyond", GoodMan Series, (Patrick Mukosha, 2024).

Figure 12: 6G Applications

In summary, with its wide range of possible uses, 6G promises to revolutionize many industries and enhance our daily lives, workplaces, and interpersonal relationships. These applications will become more specific as 6G research and development advance, resulting in breakthroughs that fully utilize the capabilities of this next-generation technology. The goal of 6G is to enable new experiences and capabilities that will influence the direction of our connected world in the future, not only to increase speeds and decrease latency.

8.8. Preparing for the 6G Future

A comprehensive approach including several aspects, such as infrastructure development, human resources, regulatory frameworks, and technology innovation, is required to get ready for the 6G future. The move from 5G to 6G represents more than just an update; rather, it represents a fundamental shift that will call for concerted efforts from a range of stakeholders, including the public, businesses, governments, and academic institutions. Here's a thorough look at how to get ready for the world of 6G:

8.8.1. **Research and Technological Innovation:**

a. **Investment in R&D**:
- **Example:** Governments and businesses in the private sector must greatly expand their financial support for 6G research projects. The Hexa-X project, for example, was started by the European Union with the goal of defining the technological roadmap and vision for 6G. To drive innovation, similar endeavors are essential.
- **Impact:** Increased financing has the potential to spur innovation in important fields including terahertz communication, sophisticated AI integration, and semiconductor and antenna novel materials.

b. **Collaborative Research:**
- **Example:** Technological developments can be accelerated by collaborative efforts among research institutes, tech enterprises, and universities. One such example is the Finnish University of Oulu's 6G Flagship program, which unites several stakeholders to investigate 6G technologies.
- **Impact:** By ensuring that a variety of skills and resources are combined, collaboration promotes innovation and improves the way that difficult technical problems are solved.

8.8.2. **Development of Infrastructure**

a. **Improvement of Current Infrastructure:**
- **Example:** 6G capabilities can be supported by gradually upgrading the current 5G infrastructure. In order to guarantee that current network architecture can support future 6G requirements, telecom operators

such as Verizon and AT&T are already making investments in network upgrades.

Impact: By optimizing current investments and anticipating future technological requirements, this strategy guarantees a more seamless transition.

b. Constructing New Infrastructure:

- **Example:** It's critical to deploy new base stations, particularly ones that can handle terahertz frequencies. Advanced base station prototypes are being developed by companies such as Huawei and Nokia in preparation for the deployment of 6G.
- **Impact:** In order to enable applications such as driverless vehicles and smart cities, 6G's ultra-low latency and high-speed capabilities will require new infrastructure.

8.8.3. Frameworks for Regulation and Policy

a. Allocation of Spectrum:

- **Example:** regulatory agencies must designate and allot spectrum bands for 6G applications. In the United States, for example, the Federal Communications Commission (FCC) is crucial to the management and auctioning off of spectrum bands that are appropriate for 6G.
- **Impact:** In order to prevent interference and guarantee the effective use of available frequencies, which permits high-speed and dependable communication, proper spectrum allocation is essential.

8.8.4. Interoperability and International Standards:

- **Example:** the development of international standards for 6G depends heavily on institutions such as the Third Generation Partnership Project (3GPP) and the International Telecommunication Union (ITU). These standards guarantee smooth operation of devices and networks around the globe.
- **Impact:** By fostering compatibility and interoperability across various manufacturers and geographical areas, standardization encourages worldwide acceptance and cooperation.

8.8.5. Development of Human Capital and Skill

a. Training and Education:

- **Example:** 6G technologies and associated subjects must be included in the updated curricula of universities and technical institutes. Programs like as the 5G/6G Innovation Centre at the University of Surrey offer students access to specialized training and research possibilities.

- **Impact:** Equipping the next generation of workers with the know-how and abilities they'll need to drive 6G innovation and deployment will guarantee a consistent flow of competent workers.

b. **Industry-University Collaborations:**

- **Example:** partnerships between businesses and educational establishments can result in internship and cooperative education programs that offer students hands-on training with state-of-the-art technologies. For example, collaborations between academic institutions and corporations such as Ericsson promote research and hands-on training in next-generation networks.
- **Impact:** By bridging the knowledge gap between theory and practice, these collaborations help students get ready for real-world obstacles in the 6G environment.

8.8.6. **Privacy and Security**

a. **Creating Robust Security Protocols:**

- **Example:** Creating sophisticated security procedures is crucial since 6G will link a huge variety of devices and systems. To safeguard 6G networks from potential quantum computing threats, organizations such as IBM and Cisco are investigating quantum-safe cryptography techniques.
- **Impact:** Making sure that strong security protocols are in place will guard against online attacks and preserve the confidentiality and integrity of data transferred across 6G networks.

b. **Standards and Regulatory Compliance:**

- **Example:** regulatory organizations must set strict policies and requirements for privacy and security. The GDPR, which was implemented by the European Union, has raised the standard for data protection, and 6G will require comparable laws.
- **Impact:** Unambiguous rules and guidelines support user confidence and guarantee that businesses follow industry best practices for protecting customer information and privacy.

8.8.7. **Economic and Social Implications:**

a. **Financial Encouragement and Assistance:**

- **Example:** governments can offer grants, tax breaks, and subsidies to businesses that invest in 6G technologies. For example, South Korea has made major investments in 6G research as part of a larger economic plan.
- **Impact:** By encouraging innovation and preserving a competitive edge in the global market, financial incentives can hasten the development and implementation of 6G technology.

b. **Taking Care of the Digital Divide:**

- **Example:** It is critical to guarantee that 6G technology is available to everyone, particularly those living in rural and underserved areas. By supporting the construction of digital infrastructure, programs like the FCC's Rural Digital Opportunity Fund seek to close the digital gap.
- **Impact:** By giving underprivileged groups chances for economic growth, healthcare, and education, inclusive access to 6G technology can support socioeconomic development.

In summary, a comprehensive strategy that takes into account technological innovation, infrastructure development, legal frameworks, skill development, security precautions, and socioeconomic factors is needed to get ready for the 6G future. Through a holistic approach, stakeholders can guarantee a seamless, effective, and advantageous shift to 6G for the greater good of society. 6G technology has the potential to completely transform many facets of our life, but fully realizing this potential will require careful planning.

8.9. Route from 5G to 6G

Wireless communication technology has advanced significantly with the shift from 5G to 6G, offering improvements in capacity, speed, latency, and connectivity. While 5G concentrates on improved mobile broadband, massive machine-type communications, and ultra-reliable low-latency communication, 6G seeks to create an intelligent, ubiquitous, and fully immersive network environment by integrating cutting-edge technologies like edge computing, machine learning, and artificial intelligence.

8.9.1. **Main Forces Behind the Development of 6G**

- **Technological Advancements:** Network optimization, autonomous management, and predictive maintenance through the integration of AI and ML.

- **Spectrum Efficiency:** Utilizing higher frequency bands, or terahertz frequencies, to reach previously unheard-of data rates and capacity is known as spectrum efficiency.
- **Network Architecture:** Use blockchain and edge computing to move toward a more intelligent and decentralized network architecture.
- **Use Cases:** Facilitating future applications like Internet of Everything (IoE), augmented and virtual reality (AR/VR) experiences, and holographic communications.

8.9.2. Important Entities in the Telecommunications Sector:

- **Nokia:** Heading up 6G research projects and working with academic institutions and research centers.
- **Ericsson:** Concentrating on 6G technology's useful applications and basic research.
- **Huawei:** In spite of geopolitical obstacles, the company is making significant investments in 6G R&D.
- **Samsung:** Contributing to standardization initiatives and actively investigating 6G use cases.

8.9.3. Tech Giants:

- **Google:** Researching edge computing applications and AI-driven network solutions.
- **Apple:** Investigating cutting-edge wireless technology for possible incorporation into upcoming products.
- **Microsoft:** Developing edge computing and cloud-based solutions to enable next-generation networks.

8.9.4. Establishments for Education and Research:

- **University of Oulu (Finland):** In charge of multiple 6G research initiatives and the home of the 6G Flagship program is the University of Oulu in Finland.
- **NYU Wireless (USA):** Leading-edge research in mmWave and terahertz communication technologies is being done at NYU Wireless (USA).
- **Tokyo Institute of Technology (Japan)** is looking into 6G gadget technology and novel materials.

8.9.5. Standards Organizations:

- **3GPP:** Essential to the creation of international standards for 5G and beyond.

- **ITU:** Promoting global collaboration and outlining the goals for IMT-2030 (6G).
- **IEEE:** Supporting standardization and research initiatives for next-generation wireless technology.

8.9.6. **Worldwide Expectations:**

8.9.6.1. **Performance Improvements**

- Data speeds higher than 1 Tbps.
- Decreased latency to a few microseconds.
- For vital applications, availability and reliability greatly increased.

8.9.7. **Environmental Impact:**

- Network procedures that save energy.
- Infrastructure that is sustainable and aims to lower carbon emissions.

8.9.8. **Economic Impact:**

- Enabling fresh revenue streams and business strategies in a range of industries.
- Generating employment in high-tech industries.

8.9.9. **Societal Impact:**

- Supplying widespread and reasonably priced internet access in order to close the digital divide.
- Improving healthcare, education, and public safety with cutting-edge applications.

8.9.10. **Challenges to Come:**

8.9.10.1. **Technical Challenges:**

- creating devices with terahertz operating frequency in mind.
- guaranteeing backward compatibility and interoperability with current networks.

8.9.10.2. **Policy and Regulatory Challenges:**

- balancing the distribution of spectrum worldwide.
- addressing security and privacy issues brought on by ubiquitous networking.

8.9.10.3. **Economic Challenges:**

- defending the enormous financial outlay needed for 6G infrastructure.
- ensuring that all communities and areas have fair access to 6G technologies.

In summary, there will be substantial changes in technology, economy, and society on the route to 6G and beyond. In order to overcome the obstacles and fully utilize 6G, cooperation between officials, academic institutions, and business leaders will be essential. The trip aims to transform how we work, live, and engage with technology, resulting in a world that is more intelligent, connected, and sustainable.

8.10. Effects on the Economy and Industry Transformation:

6G, the next generation mobile standard, gives telecoms the chance to upend the current quo and resuscitate the sector. With careful development, 6G can spur future waves of disruptive technologies, promote innovation, increase adoption, and draw in enough cross-sector investment. Most importantly, it might provide new value that telecoms can finally benefit from on top of the connectivity layer.

The need for 6G telecommunications is now more important than ever thanks to increased worldwide connectivity. The Gs, or generations of wireless cellular technology, have been increasing every ten years: before 1990, in 1990, in 2000, in 2010 at 4G, and in 2020 at 5G. The launch of 6G is anticipated for 2030. Plotting the Gs over time reveals an exponential increase in data volume, which emphasizes the demand for more advanced technical platforms. Technologists refer to this as "broadening," or "broader usage," of the frequency spectrum. A number of technologies are anticipated to come together and function in a complementary way in the development of 6G platforms. These include edge computing, next-generation satellites, the Metaverse, artificial intelligence (AI), augmented intelligence for cybersecurity, and the Internet of Everything (IoE).

The way we live and work will be further transformed by the power of data, ubiquitous high-speed connections, and computation coming together in a meaningful way. Even while technology is developing more quickly than before, the social effects are frequently overlooked.

The telecom sector must overcome the obstacles brought about by earlier generations of wireless telecommunications standards, particularly those that resulted from 5G, if it is to benefit from the potential benefits of 6G. There are many different expectations for 6G, and its future is hindered by persistent doubts about the difficulties and expenses associated with the 5G deployment. These beliefs suggest that instead of being the next big thing in technology, 6G may end up being an afterthought.

Here is an analysis of 6G's expected impact on society and the economy:

8.10.1.   Economic Impacts:

8.10.1.1. Industry Transformation

- **Industry 4.0 and Manufacturing**: 6G will make it possible for factories to become even more automated through the use of AI-driven processes, real-time data analytics, and increasingly advanced IoT devices. This will boost output and efficiency. This shift may lessen the demand for some manual labor positions while also creating high-tech opportunities.
- **Healthcare:** The ultra-low latency and great dependability of 6G will enable more sophisticated remote surgery and telemedicine. This may save healthcare expenditures and enhance public health outcomes by increasing access to high-quality healthcare in isolated and neglected areas.
- **Transportation & Logistics:** 6G's high-speed, low-latency connectivity will help autonomous cars and smart logistics networks, which will lower transportation costs and improve supply chains.

8.10.1.2. Novel Business Models:

- **Service Innovation:** New services in fields like AR/VR, digital twins, and immersive experiences will be facilitated by improved connection and data capabilities. New business opportunities and revenue streams may result from these breakthroughs.
- **Gig Economy Expansion**: With reliable 6G networks making remote work more feasible and effective, the gig economy may grow even more, providing more freedom and opening up new opportunities for freelance and distant employment.

8.10.1.3. Economic Development

- **GDP Contribution:** Through higher productivity, the opening of new markets, and the development of new technologies, the implementation of 6G technology can considerably boost GDP growth.
- **Investment Opportunities:** There will be opportunities for venture capital, private equity, and public-private partnerships as a result of significant investments in 6G infrastructure and related technologies.

8.10.2.   Social Impacts

8.10.2.1. Digital Integration:

- **Bridging the Digital Divide:** 6G intends to ensure that more people have access to the internet and digital services by bringing high-speed connectivity to even the most isolated and underprivileged locations. This will promote digital inclusion.
- **Education:** Improved connectivity will transform distance learning, offering students all over the world immersive, high-quality learning experiences and possibly even lowering educational disparities.

8.10.2.2. Quality of Life:

- **Smart Cities**: 6G will help create these cities, which will improve living circumstances for urban residents by utilizing energy more efficiently, enhancing public services, and managing traffic.
- **Health and Safety:** Better emergency response systems, enhanced health monitoring, and telemedicine services all promote public safety and raise quality of life.

8.10.2.3. Social and Cultural Dynamics:

- **Global Connectivity:** 6G will make it easier for people to communicate and work together globally, promoting understanding and cross-cultural exchange. A more cohesive and interconnected global civilization may result from this.
- **Social Interactions:** People will be able to connect in more meaningful and engaging ways, even when they are far apart, thanks to virtual and augmented reality experiences.

8.10.3. Considerations and Challenges

8.10.3.1. Inequality in the Economy:

- **Access and affordability:** Although 6G has the potential to close the gap in digital access, there is a big obstacle in making sure that it is both inexpensive and available to everyone. There's a chance that 6G's benefits won't be dispersed fairly, aggravating already-existing disparities.
- **Employment Displacement:** In some industries, the automation and efficiency improvements brought about by 6G may result in employment displacement. To lessen these effects, businesses and policymakers must concentrate on reskilling and upskilling employees.

8.10.3.2. Security and Privacy:

- **Data Privacy:** Ensuring strong data privacy and protection measures will be essential in light of the growing connectivity and data collection. To protect user data, rigorous policies and technologies are required.
- **Cybersecurity:** The significance of cybersecurity will increase as 6G networks become a necessary component of vital infrastructure. It will be crucial to defend these networks against cyberattacks in order to preserve public confidence and security.

8.10.3.3. Environmental Impact:

- **Energy Consumption:** 6G promises to be more energy-efficient, but due to the massive scope of network rollout and the rise in connected devices, overall energy consumption may increase. Green technologies and sustainable behaviors will be essential to reducing this impact.
- **E-Waste:** As technology develops more quickly, there may be more electronic garbage. To solve this problem, strategies for the recycling and environmentally friendly disposal of electronic gadgets will be required.

In summary, deep socioeconomic shifts will result from the move to 6G and beyond, altering economies, cultures, and industries. Enhanced connection has enormous potential to promote global collaboration, raise living standards, and accelerate economic progress. To fully reap the rewards of this technology revolution, it will be imperative to solve the related issues of regulating environmental repercussions, maintaining fair access, and safeguarding privacy. In order to navigate these changes and build a more inclusive, secure, and sustainable future, stakeholders from a variety of governments, businesses, and communities must collaborate.

8.11. The Progression of Technology from 5G to 6G

The number of Internet-of-Things (IoT) devices has significantly increased due to recent technical advancements, creating a new paradigm of user experiences that are unmatched. This has greatly improved a variety of creative applications, and the birth of numerous use cases has started. Better flexible communication network design that is incredibly intelligent and able to deliver lightning-fast, ultra-reliable, and low-latency communications is needed to accomplish this.

Sixth-generation (6G) communication technologies are *anticipated to satisfy these requirements of the upcoming generation of wireless communication systems*. With the completion of the fifth generation standardization procedure, the global installation has commenced. In order to maintain the competitiveness of cellular networks, business and academia have already started working together to build the next generation of communication networks, or "6G." It lays the foundation for stacking the 2030s' growing communication demands.

8.11.1. Bandwidth and Data Rate

- **5G:** Offers bandwidths from 24 GHz to 100 GHz and data speeds up to 20 Gbps.
- **6G:** Intended to use bandwidths between 100 GHz and 1 THz and reach data rates as high as 1 Tbps.
- **Example:** a 100 GB 4K movie could only take a few seconds to download over 6G as opposed to several minutes over 5G.

8.11.2. Latency

- **5G:** 1 ms is the minimum latency.
- **6G:** Aiming for latency of less than 1 ms, maybe in the region of microseconds.
- **Example:** smooth remote surgery and real-time holographic communications may become possible, significantly enhancing telepresence and healthcare applications.

8.11.3. Connectivity and Network Capacity

- **5G:** Up to one million devices per square kilometer are supported with 5G.
- **6G:** Up to 10 million devices per square kilometer are the goal of 6G.
- **Example:** smart cities could improve urban living by running more smoothly thanks to the interconnection of all infrastructure components, from waste management systems to traffic lights.

8.11.4. Integration of AI and Machine Learning

- **5G:** Simple ML and AI for network administration.
- **6G:** Sixth-generation networks will be autonomous and self-optimizing thanks to advanced AI and ML that are deeply ingrained in network operations.

- **Example:** networks might automatically adjust their configuration to maximize efficiency during periods of high traffic, guaranteeing a constant level of service quality.

8.11.5. Spectrum Usage and Efficiency

- **5G:** Makes use of upgraded spectrum sharing methods and millimeter-wave bands.
- **6G:** Terahertz waves and even more sophisticated spectrum sharing and usage are anticipated.
- **Example:** improved connectivity and increased data throughput in crowded urban areas are made possible by increased spectrum efficiency.

8.11.6. Efficiency in Energy Use

- **5G:** Energy usage improvements over earlier generations.
- **6G:** A strong emphasis on energy efficiency, maybe through the deployment of cutting-edge power-saving technologies and renewable energy sources.
- **Example:** consider lower energy usage for network operations and data centers, which helps create a greener infrastructure for technology.

8.11.7. Strengthened Privacy and Security

- **5G:** Security protocols are better than in earlier generations.
- **6G:** Even more powerful security systems, possibly with AI-powered threat detection and quantum cryptography.
- **Example:** confidential conversations and financial transactions will be safer, lowering the possibility of cyberattacks and security breaches.

8.11.8. Social and Economic Advantages of 6G

8.11.8.1. Healthcare

- **Benefit:** Better access to cutting-edge treatment via telemedicine, virtual surgery, and remote testing.
- **Example:** An example would be a New York surgeon precisely and without delay in real time executing a difficult surgery on a patient in a remote African town.

8.11.8.2. Education:

- **Benefits:** Immersion virtual reality (VR) and augmented reality (AR) provide enhanced learning opportunities by facilitating distant study with in-person engagement.

- **Example:** might be students participating in virtual lab activities or interacting with holographic depictions of historical events in classrooms.

8.11.8.3. Economic Growth and Job Creation

- **Benefit**: The demand for sophisticated technology development, implementation, and maintenance will lead to the emergence of new sectors and job possibilities.
- **Example:** the growth of 6G networks will increase the need for engineers, cybersecurity professionals, data scientists, and experts in artificial intelligence.

8.11.8.4. Smart Cities

- **Benefits:** Better energy consumption, less traffic, safer streets, and more effective urban planning and administration.
- **Example:** autonomous cars can easily interface with traffic control systems to minimize collisions and improve traffic flow.

8.11.8.5. Environmental Impact

- **Benefit**: Utilizing renewable energy sources for network operations and energy-efficient devices reduces carbon footprint.
- **Example:** data centers that use sophisticated energy management technologies to reduce power use during off-peak hours and solar energy to power themselves.

8.11.8.6. Improved Connectivity and Digital Inclusion

- **Benefit**: Improved connectivity will help close the digital gap and advance socioeconomic inclusion in distant and underdeveloped places.
- **Example:** farmers in rural locations can increase their income and productivity by using real-time market prices, weather forecasts, and agricultural advice.

In summary, significant technological breakthroughs will occur with the switch from 5G to 6G, especially in the areas of data speeds, latency, connection, AI integration, spectrum efficiency, energy efficiency, and security. These advancements will boost healthcare, education, economic growth, smart cities, environmental sustainability, and digital inclusiveness, among other socioeconomic benefits that will be far-reaching. 6G's revolutionary potential will make the globe more inclusive, efficient, and networked.

Beyond 5G is viewed as a route to 6G technology, which will take the place of fifth-generation capabilities and applications. The foundation for 6G has been laid by the numerous private wireless communications deployments of 5G for business and industrial clients, combining LTE, 5G, and edge computing. 6G wireless networks of the next generation will go one step farther in this regard. They will establish a network of communication providers, many of which will be self-suppliers, in a manner similar to how cogeneration in the Smart grid has been made possible by photovoltaic solar power. Mesh networks could benefit from 6G's advancement from conception to implementation, expanding coverage beyond the limitations of previous cell towers.

Massive 5G-driven changes are already being addressed by data centers. These include difficulties related to the simultaneous support of public and private networks, virtualization, programmable networks, and edge computing. For edge and core computing, respectively, some business clients could wish to mix on-premises RAN with hosted and hybrid on-premises computing, and data center-hosted core network components for private business networks or alternative service providers.

6G radio networks will enable the data collection and communication required to compile information. The 6G technology market, which leverages AI, data analytics, and next-generation computational power from HPC and quantum computing, requires a systems approach. 6G will bring about significant changes not just to RAN technology but also to the core communications network fabric due to the introduction of numerous new technologies. Notably, 6G will put AI front and center.

In addition, 6G is probably going to bring about the following changes:

- **Data Management:** The enormous volumes of data generated by 6G's sensing, imaging, and location-based capabilities will need to be handled on behalf of network owners, service providers, and data owners.
- **Core and Edge Synchronization:** Compared to 5G networks, 6G networks will generate a lot more data, and computing will advance to integrate edge and core platform coordination. Data centers will need to adjust in reaction to those developments.

- **Nano-Core:** It is anticipated that a shared computing core incorporating AI and HPC components will emerge as the so-called Nano-Core. It is not necessary for the Nano-Core to be a tangible network component. Alternatively, it could refer to a logical grouping of shared computational resources among numerous networks and systems.

Chapter 9: 7G Network – The Future is Here!

9.1. What is 7G Network?

With speed, latency, and connectivity improvements over 6G, the 7G (seventh generation) network is the next big thing in wireless communication technology. 7G is expected to enable extraordinary data transfer rates, ultra-low latency, and huge connection, clearing the path for revolutionary breakthroughs in both social and business applications, even if it is currently primarily hypothetical and under investigation.

9.1.1. **Benefits of 7G Network:**

9.1.1.1. **Unprecedented Speed:** Data transfer speeds in the terabits per second (Tbps) range are anticipated with 7G, which is a major increase above 6G. This would enable minimally delayed real-time communication and instantaneous data transfer.

9.1.1.2. **Ultra-Low Latency:** 7G networks may be able to achieve microsecond latency, which would allow for almost instantaneous communication. Applications that need real-time answers, like remote surgery and driverless cars, depend on this.

9.1.1.3. **Enhanced Connectivity:** In order to handle the rapidly expanding IoT (Internet of Things) market, 7G is anticipated to enable a large number of connected devices per square kilometer.

9.1.1.4. **Better Security and Dependability:** 7G networks will provide better security and dependability thanks to sophisticated authentication and encryption techniques, making them appropriate for important applications.

9.1.1.5. **Energy Efficiency:** 7G is anticipated to be more energy-efficient than previous generations, lowering the carbon impact of mobile networks and data centers even as it offers faster and greater capacity.

9.1.2. **Advantages for Society**

9.1.2.1. **Smart Cities:** 7G will make it possible to create urban areas with integrated infrastructure for public safety, energy distribution, and traffic control. Smart grids, for instance, might control the distribution of power in a dynamic manner, cutting waste and increasing effectiveness.

9.1.2.2. **Healthcare:** With 7G's low latency and great reliability, remote medical treatments and real-time health monitoring will become more practical.

Wearable technology has the potential to continuously monitor patient health and notify physicians of any irregularities.

9.1.2.3. **Education:** By enabling immersive learning experiences through augmented and virtual reality, 7G has the potential to completely transform education. No matter where they are physically located, students can take part in interactive courses and virtual field trips.

9.1.2.4. **Entertainment & Media:** It will be possible to provide improved streaming services with more engaging material and greater resolution. Users might, for example, feel as though they are in the stadium when watching live sports events in virtual reality.

9.1.3. Benefits for Business

9.1.3.1. **Industry 4.0:** Real-time monitoring and automation brought about by 7G will help manufacturing and industrial processes. Utilizing IoT devices, factories can forecast maintenance requirements and optimize production processes, cutting expenses and downtime.

9.1.3.2. **Telecommunications:** By providing innovative services and applications like increased mobile internet and immersive video calls, telecom businesses may draw in more clients and boost income.

9.1.3.3. **Financial Services:** Financial transactions can be carried out more safely and effectively thanks to 7G's enhanced security and dependability. For high-frequency trading and other time-sensitive financial processes, this is essential.

9.1.3.4. **Retail:** 7G will make shopping more engaging and individualized. Customers can virtually try on clothing or see how furniture would look in their houses by using augmented reality apps, for instance.

9.1.4. Examples

9.1.4.1. **Autonomous Vehicles:** Safe and effective operation of autonomous vehicles will depend on the low latency and high dependability of 7G networks. Improved traffic management and a decrease in accidents will be made possible by real-time communication between infrastructure and automobiles.

9.1.4.2. **Remote Surgery:** Thanks to 7G networks, surgeons may operate from a distance with accuracy and dependability. In an emergency when skilled surgeons are not physically accessible, this could save lives.

9.1.4.3. **Smart Agriculture:** 7G can enable cutting-edge farming techniques by utilizing Internet of Things (IoT) devices to track crop development, weather, and soil health. Farmers may use this data to streamline their processes, boost yields, and use less resources.

In conclusion, the 7G network's unheard-of speed, minimal latency, and extensive connectivity promise to transform both business and society. Even though it is still in the conceptual and research stages, it has enormous potential benefits that might lead to new services and uses in a variety of industries.

9.2. 7G Network's Technical Advantage Over 6G Network:

9.2.1. Faster Data Transfer Rates

- **6G:** 1 terabit per second (Tbps) of data transfer speeds are anticipated.
- **7G:** Data transfer speeds might potentially reach multiple terabits per second, expected to eclipse 6G.
- **Example:** For instance, a 4K video could only take a few milliseconds to download over a 7G network as opposed to several seconds or minutes over a 6G network.

9.2.2. Extremely Low Latency

- **6G:** Aims for latency of one millisecond or less.
- **7G:** Sub-millisecond latency (microseconds) is the target.
- **Example:** A 7G network could improve safety and coordination in autonomous driving by enabling nearly instantaneous real-time vehicle-to-vehicle communication and decision-making.

9.2.3. Improved Use of Spectrum

- **6G:** For more bandwidth, sub-terahertz frequencies (100 GHz to 1 THz) are used.
- **7G:** For even more bandwidth and data speeds, it is anticipated to investigate higher frequencies, such as the terahertz range (1 THz and upwards).
- **Example:** An illustration of this would be exceptionally high-density user situations, such as stadiums or concerts, when thousands of devices are in simultaneous need of high-speed connections.

9.2.4. Better Density and Connectivity

- **6G:** Up to 10 million linked devices per square kilometer are expected to be supported by 6G.

- **7G:** This density is expected to expand dramatically with 7G, which would enable hundreds of millions of devices per square kilometer.
- **Example:** As an illustration, 7G might provide smooth connectivity for a vast network of sensors, cameras, and Internet of Things (IoT) devices in a smart city, guaranteeing effective municipal administration and enhanced public services.

9.2.5. Advanced Integration of Machine Learning and AI

- **6G:** AI is incorporated for resource management and network optimization.
- **7G:** Will enable autonomous network management, predictive maintenance, and real-time analytics by pushing AI integration to new heights.
- **Example:** As an illustration, a 7G network might manage and optimize itself on its own using real-time data, cutting down on downtime and enhancing network performance overall without the need for human interaction.

9.2.6. Sustainability and Energy Efficiency

- **6G:** This technology aims to boost energy efficiency, but it still has issues with higher power consumption as a result of faster data rates and greater connectivity.
- **7G:** Intended to make use of cutting-edge materials and energy-saving technology to achieve increased energy efficiency while maintaining improved performance.
- **Example:** For instance, data centers running on 7G networks might require a great deal less energy to run, which would have a negative effect on the environment and operational expenses.

9.2.7. Improvements in Security

- **6G:** Offers strong security protections, yet it could still be open to new online dangers.
- **7G:** Designed to fend off sophisticated cyberattacks, it will include other state-of-the-art security features along with powerful quantum encryption.
- **Example:** By utilizing 7G networks, financial organizations can carry out transactions with higher security and safeguard sensitive data from risks posed by quantum computing.

9.2.8. Examples of Applications for 7G Superiority

9.2.8.1. Holographic Communication

- **6G:** Enables basic augmented reality (AR) apps and high-definition video conversations.
- **7G:** Provides full-resolution, real-time holographic communication, enabling immersive virtual meetings and exchanges.
- **Example:** For instance, companies may hold virtual meetings where attendees are represented by lifelike holograms, improving cooperation and cutting down on travel.

9.2.8.2. Remote Medical Procedures

- **6G:** With certain restrictions owing to latency and data transfer rates, 6G enables remote surgery.
- **7G**: Offers the extremely low latency and excellent dependability needed for accurate, real-time remote surgical operations.
- **Example:** By enhancing access to healthcare, a specialized surgeon could precisely execute complex surgeries on patients in faraway regions with the same level of accuracy as if they were present in person.

9.2.8.3. Smart Grids

- **6G:** Offers some real-time capabilities along with basic smart grid control.
- **7G:** Enables extremely responsive and dynamic smart grids that can instantly adjust to variations in the supply and demand for electricity.
- **Example:** As an illustration, utility firms might employ 7G networks to instantly balance loads, improving the integration of renewable energy sources and lowering the frequency of power outages.

In summary, with its technical superiority over 6G in a number of areas, including data transfer rates, latency, connectivity density, AI integration, energy efficiency, and security, the 7G network is expected to represent a significant advancement in wireless communication. These developments will improve current conditions and create new ones.

9.3. A Roadmap for The 7G Network

There are multiple phases of research, development, standardization, and implementation involved in the transition from 5G to 7G. Every successive generation of wireless technology improves on the one before it, bringing in new features and solving new problems. A thorough roadmap outlining the important checkpoints and procedures needed to get from 5G to 7G is provided below.

9.3.1. **5G Evolution**

9.3.1.1. **The Current State (2024):**

- **Deployment:** 5G networks are being widely installed throughout the world, covering a large number of countries.
- **Capabilities:** 5G enables applications including enhanced mobile broadband, edge computing, and the Internet of Things by providing fast data transfer rates, low latency, and the capacity to link a huge number of devices.

9.3.1.2. **Next Actions:**

- **Optimization:** Boost the performance of the 5G network by using network densification, software upgrades, and cutting-edge antenna technologies (such Massive MIMO).
- **Extension:** Bring 5G service to underserved and rural locations.
- **Use Case Development:** Create and market novel use cases, such as remote healthcare, driverless cars, and smart cities.

9.3.2. **Research and Development for 6G**

- **Timeline: 2023–2028**
- **Research Initiatives:** To investigate 6G technologies and applications, governments, academic institutions, and industry consortiums launch research projects.
- **Principal Topics of Interest:**
  - **Communication in Terahertz (THz):** Utilize higher frequency ranges to achieve extremely high data rates.
  - **AI/ML Advanced Integration:** Improve network automation, optimization, and management with advanced AI/ML integration.
  - **New hardware and Material:** Develop cutting-edge semiconductors and nanotechnology to improve performance and energy efficiency. Create new materials and devices.
  - **Quantum Communication:** Examine secure data transport techniques and quantum encryption in the context of quantum communication.
- **Attempts toward Standardization:**

- o **ITU and 3GPP:** Start developing the 6G technical specifications and standards.
- o **Industry Cooperation:** Work together with interested parties to guarantee consensus and worldwide interoperability.

9.3.3. Early 6G Trials and Development

- **Timeline: 2025–2030:**
- **Testing and Prototyping:** Create early 6G technology prototypes and carry out field tests to confirm viability and performance.
- **Use Case Exploration:** Locate and evaluate prospective 6G uses, such as enhanced IoT scenarios, holographic communication, and immersive AR/VR.
- **Allocating Spectrum:** Assist regulatory agencies in allocating the appropriate spectrum bands for the deployment of 6G.

9.3.4. Commercial Sixth Wave Deployment

- **Timeline: 2030–2035:**
- **Initial Rollout:** In urban and high-demand areas, start the commercial deployment of 6G networks.
- **Device Ecosystem:** Introduce sensors and devices that are 6G compatible to enable new services and use cases.
- **Network Evolution:** To improve coverage and performance, keep growing and optimizing 6G networks.

9.3.5. 7G Research and Development

- **Timeline: 2035–2040:**
- **Next-Generation Research:** Expanding on the developments and knowledge gained from 6G, begin research on 7G technology.
- **Principal Topics of Interest:**
  - o **Hyper-Connectivity:** Support even more connected devices per square kilometer with hyper-connectivity.
  - o **Ultra-Low latency and Reliability:** Microsecond-level latency and improved network dependability are the goals of ultra-low latency and reliability.
  - o **Energy Efficiency:** Create environmentally friendly materials and technology to use less energy.
  - o **Advanced Security:** Use encryption that is resistant to quantum rays and other cutting-edge security techniques.

- **Attempts toward Standardization:**
  - o **ITU and 3GPP:** Establish technical guidelines and requirements for 7G.
  - o **Industry Cooperation:** Take part in international cooperation to guarantee 7G standard consensus and compatibility.

9.3.6. Initial 7G Development and Trials

- **Timelines: 2040–2045:**
- **Testing and Prototyping:** Create early 7G technology prototypes and carry out comprehensive field tests.
- **Use Case Exploration:** Determine and evaluate possible uses for 7G, including sophisticated smart cities, remote operations in real time, and interfaces for communication beyond human capabilities.
- **Spectrum Allocation:** Collaborate with regulatory agencies to assign the appropriate spectrum bands for the rollout of 7G.

9.3.7. Commercial 7G Deployment:

- **Timeline: 2045–2050:**
- **First Rollout:** Start the commercial rollout of 7G networks with an emphasis on urban areas and strong demand.
- **Device Ecosystem:** Introduce sensors and devices that are compatible with 7G, opening up new applications and services.
- **Network Evolution:** Keep improving and growing 7G networks to improve coverage, speed, and interoperability with earlier generations.

In summary, the 7G roadmap consists of a sequence of small-scale innovations and developments that expand upon the 5G and 6G foundations. It includes thorough research and development, exacting standards procedures, and deployment plans that are phased in. By adhering to this roadmap, the industry hopes to provide revolutionary wireless communication technologies that will revolutionize business and society, solve upcoming issues, and open up new avenues.

Conclusion

a. **The Evolution of Interconnectivity**
   - **Historical Background:** Every generation of wireless technology, from 1G's early days to 5G's revolutionary potential, has dramatically improved our ability to connect and communicate with one another and the outside world.
   - **5G Advancements:** 5G has ushered in a new era of connectivity by bringing high-speed data transfer, low latency, and the ability to link a large number of devices.

b. **Key Characteristics and Advantages of 5G's Increased Capacity and Speed:**
   - Enhanced Speed and Capacity: With speeds up to 100 times quicker than 4G, 5G networks allow for smooth streaming, quick downloads, and real-time communication.
   - **Low Latency:** 5G's extremely low latency enables real-time applications like augmented reality, remote surgery, and autonomous driving.
   - **Massive Internet of Things Connectivity:** The capacity to link billions of IoT devices, enabling smart cities, sophisticated manufacturing, and effective energy management, which is revolutionizing industries.

c. **The Journey to 6G: Prospects for the Future**
   - **Never before seen Speed and Capacity:** 6G is anticipated to provide even reduced latency and speeds up to 1000 times faster than 5G, creating new opportunities for data-intensive applications.
   - **Holographic Communications:** Real-time holographic telepresence will transform distant communication and add realism to virtual gatherings.
   - **Advanced Artificial Intelligence Integration:** AI-powered edge computing and network management will improve security, optimize performance, and make predictive maintenance possible.

d. **Potential Progress in 6G**
   - **Healthcare:** improved telemedicine, remote procedures with incredibly dependable connection, and real-time patient monitoring.

- **Autonomous Vehicles:** Enhanced safety and efficiency through fully autonomous transportation systems that feature real-time vehicle-to-vehicle communication.
- **Immersive Extended Reality** refers to sophisticated AR, VR, and MR experiences that offer immersive and interactive worlds for training, education, and entertainment.
- **Smart Cities** are made possible by integrating millions of IoT devices to optimize energy use, traffic control, and public safety while also creating responsive urban landscapes.
- **Global Connectivity:** High-altitude platform stations (HAPS) and satellite technology will bridge the digital divide by offering high-speed internet access to all.

e. **Getting Ready for the 6G Future**:

- **Technological Innovation:** a rise in R&D spending with an emphasis on terahertz communication, AI integration, and novel materials for semiconductors and antennas of the future.
- **Infrastructure Development** is the process of creating new systems to support 6G requirements and upgrading the current 5G infrastructure.
- **Regulatory Frameworks:** Creating international guidelines and standards for security, interoperability, and spectrum distribution.
- **Human Capital:** Maintaining industry-academia collaborations and updating curricula to prepare a workforce with the necessary skills.
- **Security and Privacy:** Ensuring strong data privacy safeguards and putting modern security processes into place to guard against new cyberthreats.
- **Economic and Social Implications:** addressing the socioeconomic effects, guaranteeing fair access to technology, and offering financial incentives for 6G development.

f. **The Function of the IT Sector**

- **Promoting Innovation:** Businesses need to take the lead in R&D initiatives and push the limits of new technology's potential.
- **Cooperation:** Joining forces with government agencies, businesses, and academic institutions to promote creativity and tackle difficult problems.
- **Regulation and Standardization:** Taking an active role in the creation of international frameworks for regulations and standards to guarantee the smooth operation and integration of new technology.

- **Workforce Development:** Putting money into educational and training initiatives to produce the upcoming generation of tech workers is known as workforce development.

In summary, our digital world is expected to undergo a transformation due to the developments in 5G and upcoming 6G, which will fuel future connectivity. We can open up new opportunities, improve global connectivity, and build a more inclusive, productive, and connected world by utilizing these technologies. The tech sector needs to welcome this new era with creativity, teamwork, and a dedication to getting ready for all the possibilities and challenges that lie ahead.

C2. The Ongoing Evolution of Connectivity

The transition from 1G to 5G has resulted in unparalleled progress in wireless communication, fundamentally altering our methods of connecting, exchanging information, and engaging with the outside world. It is evident that the evolution of connectivity is far from over as we approach the 6G era. Every technological generation has improved upon the one before it, raising the bar for what can be accomplished and strengthening capabilities.

- **Opening Up New Opportunities:** With incredibly fast speeds, extremely low latency, and enormous connection, 6G promises to revolutionize connectivity. Numerous prospective uses will be made possible by this, including fully driverless transportation systems, immersive extended reality experiences, real-time holographic communication, and enhanced healthcare. The capabilities of 6G will be further enhanced by the integration of AI, quantum communication, and improved network slicing, establishing it as a pillar of the digital future.
- **Joint Ventures for Innovation:** In order to achieve 6G, industry leaders, academic institutions, governmental organizations, and regulatory authorities must work together. Making large R&D investments and forming strategic alliances will be essential to fostering innovation and resolving the technical obstacles related to 6G. Collaborative research projects like the 6G Flagship program at the University of Oulu and the EU's Hexa-X project are prime examples of the kind of cooperation required to push the envelope of what is achievable.
- **Constructing the Infrastructure:** Significant improvements to current infrastructure and the creation of new systems that can meet the needs of next-

generation connection are also necessary to get ready for 6G. Governments, telecom carriers, and tech firms must collaborate to guarantee that the required infrastructure is in place. In order to do this, new base stations must be installed, existing networks must be optimized, and strong cybersecurity must be maintained.

- **Enabling International Law and Regulations:** Global standards and regulatory frameworks are essential to the successful implementation of 6G. The development and harmonization of standards that guarantee interoperability and flawless operation across various locations and devices is greatly aided by organizations like as the ITU and 3GPP. Regulatory compliance and efficient spectrum allocation are essential for managing the new frequency bands and guaranteeing resource efficiency.

- **Getting the Workforce Ready:** The move to 6G will also necessitate the need for a trained labor force with the ability to create, deploy, and maintain cutting-edge technologies. Institutions of higher learning must modify their curricula to incorporate 6G technologies, and collaborations between industry and academics can offer chances for research and hands-on training. For the industry to continue growing and innovating, it is imperative that the next generation of scientists, engineers, and IT specialists be prepared.

- **Examining the Social and Economic Consequences:** With 6G, underserved and isolated communities could benefit from high-speed connectivity, thereby closing the digital divide. Ensuring fair access to 6G technology can facilitate social inclusion, advance socioeconomic development, and increase access to healthcare and education. In order to guarantee that the advantages of 6G are widely distributed, governments and international organizations need to give priority to these endeavors.

- **The Prospects of Connectivity:** Building on the foundations set by earlier generations, the continuous development of 6G promises a revolutionary leap forward in the evolution of connectivity. Realizing the full potential of 6G will need the concerted efforts of several stakeholders, strategic investments, and progressive policies as we get ready for this future. The way we live, work, and interact is going to be completely transformed by this new era of connectedness, creating a more connected and sophisticated world for coming generations.

As we anticipate the 6G age, it is clear that connectivity has enormous potential to change many parts of our life in the future. The breakthroughs that 6G promises—ultra-high speeds, ultra-low latency, and unmatched connectivity—are not merely little tweaks; rather, they represent fundamental changes that will completely change the way we engage with technology and one another.

- **The Potential for Groundbreaking Innovations:** Beyond the capabilities of 5G, 6G is expected to unleash technologies that will allow for the seamless integration of billions of IoT devices, real-time holographic communications, driverless mobility, and enhanced telemedicine. These developments will boost already-existing sectors, launch new ones, and provide answers to some of the most important problems facing humanity.
- **The Value of Investment and Cooperation**: It will take hitherto unheard-of levels of cooperation between academic institutions, business executives, governmental organizations, and regulatory bodies to realize the 6G ambition. Considerable funds must be allocated to research and development in order to propel the technological advancements required for 6G. Initiatives such as the University of Oulu's 6G Flagship and the EU's Hexa-X demonstrate the kind of teamwork that will be essential on this path.
- **Developing the Infrastructure for the Future**: In order to be ready for 6G, it is also necessary to upgrade current systems and install new, advanced ones that can meet the needs of next-generation connectivity. To guard against new dangers, this entails not just improving the physical infrastructure but also putting strong cybersecurity safeguards in place. Businesses that are already leading the way in the development of these technologies include Ericsson, Nokia, and Huawei.
- **Creating International Laws and Standards**: International standards and legal frameworks will be essential to the effective implementation of 6G. Establishing and harmonizing standards that guarantee compatibility and flawless operation across many locations and devices is a task for organizations like as the ITU and 3GPP. Regulatory compliance and efficient spectrum allocation are critical to managing the new frequency bands and guaranteeing resource efficiency.
- **Getting the Staff Ready for the Future**: The move to 6G will necessitate new knowledge and abilities. Institutions of higher learning must modify their curricula

to incorporate 6G technologies, and collaborations between industry and academics can offer chances for research and hands-on training. In order to maintain growth and innovation in the sector, it is imperative that the next generation of scientists, engineers, and IT professionals be prepared.

- **Resolving Socio-Economic Issues**: With 6G, underserved and isolated communities could benefit from high-speed connectivity, thereby closing the digital divide. Ensuring fair access to 6G technology may encourage social inclusion, advance socioeconomic development, and increase access to healthcare and education. To guarantee that the advantages of 6G are widely distributed, governments and international organizations need to give their efforts top priority.
- **The Future of Connectivity:**
  - **A Revolutionary Advancement**: The switch to 6G is a revolutionary step that will completely reshape our digital environment, not merely a technological improvement. The realization of the full potential of this initiative will require the cooperative efforts of several parties, wise investments, and progressive legislation. It is certain that 6G will improve connection while also reshaping the globe to make it more inclusive, efficient, and connected for coming generations as we get ready for this future.

By seizing the opportunities presented by 6G, we are entering a new era of connectivity that will transform the way we work, live, and interact, opening the door to a more promising and connected future.

Appendix:

- **Latency:** The amount of time a device takes over a network to reply to other devices. One of 5G's main promises is faster response times, which might be essential for applications like self-driving cars and emergency warning systems.
- **Spectrum:** The entire range of radio wave frequencies, spanning from 300 GHz to 3 kHz, the lowest frequency. To stop users from interfering with one another's signals, the FCC controls which bands, or ranges, of frequencies, can be used.
- **Unlicensed Spectrum:** Spectrum that isn't owned by a certain carrier, such the frequencies now in use for Wi-Fi at homes. Carriers intend to add service provided on unlicensed bands to complement their licensed spectrum.
- **Network Slicing:** The process of dividing an infrastructure carrier into "virtual networks," each with distinct characteristics. For instance, smartphones might connect to a network designed for streaming video, whereas cars might connect to a virtual network where the goal is to minimize latency.
- **Low-Band Frequencies:** Traditionally utilized by mobile networks, broadcast radio, and television, these bands below 1 GHz may readily carry over long distances and through walls, but due to their current overcrowding, carriers are moving to the higher end of the radio spectrum.
- **Mid-Band Spectrum:** Bluetooth, Wi-Fi, mobile networks, and numerous more applications use the portion of the wireless spectrum between 1 and 6 GHz. Carriers find it appealing because it provides a large amount of capacity with less obstacles than the millimeter-wave spectrum.
- **Flexible Numerology:** The capacity to allocate lower bandwidth requirements to low-demanding devices, including sensors. While not connected to the notion that numbers have esoteric significance, it can sound equally mysterious.
- **Millimeter Wave:** Depending on who you ask, the portion of the wireless spectrum above 24 or 30 GHz. This portion of the spectrum has a plenty of bandwidth, allowing carriers to reach substantially quicker speeds. However, at extended distances, millimeter-wave signals lose reliability.

Here are commonly asked questions concerning 5G, coupled with thorough responses that, when appropriate, include striking examples:

1. **5G: What is it?**
   - **Answer:** *The fifth generation mobile network is known as 5G. Following 1G, 2G, 3G, and 4G networks, it is a new global wireless standard. 5G makes possible a brand-new type of network intended to link almost everyone and everything, including devices, machines, and things. The goals of 5G wireless technology are to provide more users with more consistent user experiences, ultra-low latency, vast network capacity, faster multi-Gbps peak data speeds, and increased reliability. New user experiences are empowered and new industries are connected by increased performance and efficiency.*

2. **Who is the inventor of 5G?**
   - **Answer:** *A number of businesses across the mobile ecosystem worked to make 5G a reality, but no one corporation or individual owns 5G. This includes Ericsson, Nokia, Huawei, Qualcomm and Samsung. 3G Partnership Project (3GPP), is the driving force behind the establishment of global standards for 3G UMTS (including HSPA), 4G LTE, and 5G technologies. Several key innovations in 5G design, from the service layer to the air interface, are being driven by 3GPP. Mobile network operators, vertical service providers, infrastructure vendors, and device/component makers are among the other 3GPP 5G members.*

3. **How does 5G operate?**
   - **Answer:** *5G is built on the same mobile networking technologies as 4G LTE and uses orthogonal frequency-division multiplexing, or OFDM. But OFDM will be further improved by the new 5G NR (New Radio) air interface, which will offer a far greater level of flexibility and scalability. In addition to providing faster and better mobile broadband services than 4G LTE, 5G will open up new service opportunities including mission-critical communications and linking the vast Internet of Things. Numerous novel 5G NR air interface*

design strategies, including a unique self-contained TDD sub-frame design, make this possible.

4. **In comparison to 4G, how fast is 5G?**
    - **Answer:** *While 4G commonly peaks at 1 Gbps, 5G can reach speeds of up to 10 Gbps. This indicates that 5G has the potential to be up to ten times quicker than 4G, allowing for seamless gaming, rapid downloading of huge files, and streaming of high-definition video.*

5. **What is latency, and how is it enhanced by 5G?**
    - **Answer:** *The time it takes for data to move from one place to another is known as latency. Compared to 4G, which had latency of about 50 milliseconds, 5G has latency as low as 1 millisecond. For real-time applications such as remote surgery or autonomous driving, this enhancement is essential.*

6. **Which frequencies are used by 5G?**
    - **Answer:** *5G uses three different frequency bands to function: high-band (beyond 24 GHz), mid-band (1-6 GHz), and low-band (below 1 GHz). Broad coverage is provided by low-band, speed and coverage are balanced by mid-band, and very high speeds over short distances are delivered by high-band (millimeter wave).*

7. **What effects might 5G have on the Internet of Things (IoT)?**
    - **Answer:** *5G is perfect for Internet of Things applications because of its great reliability and low latency while connecting a large number of devices. 5G will have a big impact on linked cars, smart homes, industrial automation, and smart cities.*

8. **Can home broadband be replaced by 5G?**
    - **Answer:** *Yes, 5G can provide comparable speeds and reliability to traditional home broadband in certain areas. This is especially true in places where fiber or cable internet is either unavailable or too costly to implement.*

9. **In 5G, What Is Network Slicing?**

- **Answer:** *Multiple virtual networks can be created inside a single physical 5G network thanks to network slicing. Each slice can be customized to match the unique requirements of various applications, for example, one slice for essential medical data transfer and another for high-speed gaming.*

10. **Is 5G security compliant?**
    - **Answer:** *It is safe to use 5G, yes. It functions in the non-ionizing radio frequency range, which is too weak to harm DNA or cells. The World Health Organization (WHO) and other health organizations have conducted extensive studies and have not discovered any negative health impacts from exposure to 5G frequencies.*

11. **What difficulties are ahead for 5G deployment?**
    - **Answer:** *The necessity of large infrastructure investments, the requirement for numerous small cell sites (particularly for high-band frequencies), problems with spectrum allocation, and maintaining cybersecurity and data privacy are some of the challenges.*

12. **How does 5G help self-driving cars?**
    - **Answer:** *Real-time communication between vehicles and infrastructure (V2X) is made possible by 5G's low latency and high dependability, and it is essential for the safe operation of autonomous vehicles. This makes it possible to get real-time information on traffic, road conditions, and other vehicle movements.*

13. **What part does smart cities play for 5G?**
    - **Answer:** *5G's high capacity, low latency, and capacity to connect multiple IoT devices enable smart city applications such as intelligent traffic control, energy-efficient buildings, real-time surveillance, and improved public services.*

14. **What fundamental technology underlie 5G?**
    - **Answer:** *The foundation of 5G is orthogonal frequency-division multiplexing, or OFDM. This technique modulates a digital transmission over many channels in order to minimize interference. 5G employs OFDM concepts in addition to the 5G NR air interface. Wider bandwidth technologies like*

mmWave and sub-6 GHz are also used by 5G. 5G OFDM functions using the same mobile networking concepts as 4G LTE. Nonetheless, OFDM can be further improved by the new 5G NR air interface to provide a far greater level of flexibility and scalability. For a range of use cases, this might provide more people and things access to 5G.

Broader bandwidths will be available with 5G as it increases the use of spectrum resources from sub-3 GHz, which was employed in 4G, to 100 GHz and higher. Extreme capacity, multi-Gbps speed, and low latency will be provided by 5G, which can operate in both lower bands (such as sub-6 GHz) and mmWave (such as 24 GHz and higher). In addition to providing faster and better mobile broadband services than 4G LTE, 5G is intended to open up new service opportunities including mission-critical communications and linking the vast Internet of Things. Numerous novel 5G NR air interface design strategies, including a unique self-contained TDD sub-frame design, make this possible.

15. How will mobile gaming be impacted by 5G?

- **Answer:** *By decreasing latency, enabling cloud gaming services, and offering a more immersive, fluid gaming experience, 5G's fast speeds and low latency will improve mobile gaming. High definition games don't require downloads or updates for players to play.*

16. What makes Wi-Fi 6 and 5G different from each other?

- **Answer:** *Wi-Fi 6 and 5G are complimentary technology. Wide-area coverage is offered by 5G mobile network technology, whereas high-speed internet can be accessed within homes, offices, and public hotspots via Wi-Fi 6.*

17. In what ways does 5G improve virtual and augmented reality?

- **Answer:** *Smooth, real-time experiences in AR and VR apps are made possible by 5G's high bandwidth and low latency. For instance, students can interact with 3D models in a virtual classroom.*

18. What kind of infrastructure is required to implement 5G?

- **Answer:** *In order to implement 5G, it will be necessary to upgrade current cell towers, install new small cells (particularly for high-band frequencies), and* make sure the backhaul links are reliable. 5G base stations are frequently connected to the core network via fiber-optic connections._

19. Could a smartphone from today use 5G?

- **Answer:** *5G networks are only compatible with smartphones that have modems that can handle 5G. Although the majority of recently released flagship models from companies such as Apple, Samsung, and Google are compatible with 5G, older models cannot be used with 5G services.*

20. How does artificial intelligence (AI) function in 5G networks?

- **Answer:** *Artificial Intelligence contributes to 5G network optimization through traffic management, maintenance demand prediction, security enhancement, and resource allocation efficiency. AI can also help with real-time decision-making for a variety of applications and dynamic network slicing.*

21. How will 5G affect medical services?

- **Answer:** *5G will transform healthcare by making telemedicine, real-time patient monitoring, and remote surgery possible. For instance, surgeons can use robotic arms operated by a 5G network to operate on patients remotely.*

22. What 5G security issues are there?

- **Answer:** *5G networks' greater complexity and connectedness create security risks, including larger attack surfaces and possible weaknesses in Internet of Things devices. It is essential to have strong authentication, encryption, and network monitoring.*

23. How are emergency services improved by 5G?

- **Answer:** *By enabling dependable connectivity, instantaneous data exchange, and enhanced situational awareness, 5G improves emergency services. Drones and wearable technology, for example, can help first responders analyze the scene and coordinate activities more efficiently after a crisis.*

24. Is 5G compatible with rural areas?

- **Answer:** *Rural locations may see a slower pace of 5G implementation because of the higher expenses and lower population density. But low-band 5G can close the digital divide in these areas by improving internet access and expanding coverage.*

25. In 5G, what is beamforming?

- **Answer:** *In 5G, beamforming is a technology that focuses signals on individual users instead of dispersing them over the network. As a result, interference is decreased, signal strength is increased, and network efficiency is raised overall.*

26. How does Industry 4.0 benefit from 5G?

- **Answer:** *By enabling predictive maintenance, improved automation, and real-time monitoring and management of industrial operations, 5G helps Industry 4.0. For instance, 5G can be used in industries to connect machinery, robotics, and sensors for more effective operations.*

27. What effects does 5G have on the environment?

- **Answer:** *5G has conflicting effects on the environment. Although the deployment of more small cells and base stations may result in higher energy consumption, 5G's efficiency and compatibility with smart technology can lower overall energy consumption and emissions across a range of industries.*

28. How does video streaming get better with 5G?

- **Answer:** *5G's fast speeds and low latency improve video streaming by allowing 4K and high definition video playing and cutting down on buffering periods. Even in busy spaces, users can experience flawless streaming.*

29. What is the function of massive MIMO in 5G?

- **Answer:** *Massive MIMO (Many Input Multiple Output) base stations employ many antennas to send and receive more data at the same time. In 5G networks, this technique boosts spectral efficiency, expands coverage, and expands capacity.*

30. How does network congestion get handled with 5G?

- **Answer:** *In order to control network congestion, 5G employs cutting-edge methods such Massive MIMO, Beamforming, and Network Slicing. These techniques guarantee economical resource consumption while maintaining a constant level of service quality, especially during periods of high demand.*

31. What are 5G's financial advantages?

- **Answer:** *Significant economic growth is anticipated as a result of 5G's ability to support new business models, increase productivity, and generate employment. 5G technology will have a significant positive impact on sectors like manufacturing, healthcare, and entertainment.*

32. How will 5G impact working remotely?

- **Answer:** *By enabling seamless access to cloud-based apps and services from any place, supporting high-quality video conferencing, and offering quicker and more dependable internet connections, 5G will enhance remote work.*

33. What distinguishing features set 5G SA apart from 5G NSA?

- **Answer:** *For some purposes, 5G NSA (Non-Standalone) uses the current 4G infrastructure, offering a path to 5G in transition. With the usage of a brand-new, dedicated 5G core network, 5G SA (Standalone) provides all the advantages of 5G, such as reduced latency and network slicing.*

34. What makes 5G superior to 4G?

- **Answer:** *A number of factors indicate that 5G will outperform 4G:*
  - *It has a significantly lower latency than 4G.*
  - *It is quicker than 4G by a substantial margin.*
  - *It is more capacious than 4G.*
  - *5G is a unified platform that is more powerful than 4G.*
  - *It uses spectrum more efficiently than 4G.*
  - *5G is far much faster than 4G. With peak data rates of up to 20 gigabits per second (Gbps) and average data rates of more than 100 megabits per second (Mbps), 5G has the potential to be far faster than 4G. 5G makes better utilization of spectrum than 4G.*
  - *In addition, 5G is built to maximize utilization of all available spectrum over a broad range of spectrum regulatory regimes and bands,*

including high bands referred to as millimeter wave (mmWave), mid bands spanning from 1 GHz to 6 GHz, and low bands below 1 GHz.

- o *Compared to 4G, 5G is a more capable unified platform. While 5G is intended to be a unified, more capable platform that not only enhances mobile broadband experiences but also enables new services like mission-critical communications and the enormous Internet of Things, 4G LTE was concentrated on providing far faster mobile broadband services than 3G.*
- o *Additionally, 5G can natively handle a wide range of deployment patterns, from hotspots to classic macro-cells, as well as new interconnecting methods like device-to-device and multi-hop mesh, and all spectrum kinds, including licensed, shared, unlicensed, and bands, low, mid, and high. Over 4G, 5G has greater capacity. Over 4G, 5G has greater capacity.*
- o *A 100x improvement in traffic capacity and network efficiency is what 5G is intended to enable. 5G is less latency-prone than 4G. With a 10x reduction in end-to-end latency to 1 ms, 5G offers more rapid, real-time access with far less delay.*

35. What areas are using 5G?

- • **Answer:** *In general, 5G is utilized for three primary categories of linked services: enormous IoT, mission-critical communications, and improved mobile broadband. The capacity to handle future services that are not yet known is known as forward compatibility, and it is one of the distinguishing features of 5G.*
  - o *Massive IoT: 5G aims to provide incredibly lean and affordable connectivity solutions by seamlessly connecting a vast number of embedded sensors in almost everything by scaling down data speeds, power, and mobility.*
  - o *Mission-Critical Communications: With ultra-reliable, accessible, low-latency connectivity, 5G can open up new services like remote control of vital infrastructure, automobiles, and medical procedures that have the potential to completely change industries.*
  - o *Improved mobile internet access: 5G mobile technology can bring in new immersive experiences like VR and AR with faster, more consistent*

data rates, lower latency, and cheaper cost-per-bit, in addition to improving our devices.

1. **What are the main purposes and aims of 6G?**
    - **Question: What are the main technological objectives of 6G, and how are they different from those of 5G?**
    - **Answer:** To put it briefly, the main objectives of 6G are:
        - **Ultra-High Data Rates:** Compared to 5G, this technology can achieve data rates of up to 1 Tbps.
        - **Ultra-Low Latency:** This refers to cutting latency down to microsecond levels, which is crucial for real-time applications such as driverless cars and remote surgery.
        - **Massive Connectivity:** Enabling the Internet of Everything (IoE) by supporting an enormous number of linked devices (up to 10 million devices per square kilometer).
        - **AI Integration:** Using machine learning and AI to optimize networks, perform preventive maintenance, and run autonomously.
        - **Energy Efficiency:** Improving energy economy to facilitate environmentally friendly network operations.
        - **Reliability and Security:** Enhancing network security and dependability in order to enable vital applications.

2. **What effects would 6G have on the current network infrastructure?**
    - **Question: What alterations or additions to the current network infrastructure will be required to accommodate 6G?**
    - **Answer:** In order to facilitate 6G, the current network infrastructure needs to:
        - **New Technology:** Changing to more advanced technology that can process data at terahertz frequencies and speeds.
        - **Advanced Software:** Putting complex software into practice for AI-driven network optimization and administration.
        - **Edge Computing:** Increasing the infrastructure for edge computing can lower latency and boost the effectiveness of data processing.

- **Fiber Optics:** Expanding fiber optic networks to accommodate growing needs for backhaul.
- **Decentralized design:** To enable distributed processing and storage, a more decentralized network design is being adopted.

3. **What possible applications and use cases does 6G have?**
   - **Question: What new uses and sectors of the economy would 6G technology support?**
   - **Answer:** In response, the following are possible applications and use cases for 6G:
     - **Holographic Communication:** Facilitating immersive virtual meetings and real-time holographic video chats.
     - **Extended Reality (XR):** Enhanced AR/VR experiences with real-time interaction for training, education, and gaming are provided by extended reality (XR).
     - **Smart Cities:** Enabling smart city applications like as increased public safety systems, energy-efficient structures, and intelligent traffic management.
     - **Telemedicine:** Enhancing the provision of remote medical care by utilizing real-time remote procedures and high-resolution medical imaging.
     - **Autonomous Systems:** Using ultra-reliable low-latency communication to improve the efficiency and security of autonomous cars, drones, and robotics.

4. **What are the difficulties and roadblocks in the creation and application of 6G?**
   - **Question: What are the main economic, regulatory, and technical obstacles in the way of 6G adoption?**
   - **Answer:** In response, the following are major obstacles to the creation and implementation of 6G:
     - **Technical challenges** include managing the growing complexity of network operations, guaranteeing interoperability with current networks, and developing hardware that can operate at terahertz frequencies.

- o **Regulatory Challenges:** Creating standards for 6G technologies, resolving privacy and security issues, and harmonizing spectrum allocation globally.
- o **Economic challenges** include controlling the cost of deployment in remote and underserved areas, guaranteeing equal access to 6G technology, and justifying the enormous investment needed for 6G infrastructure.

5. **How will 6G handle sustainability and environmental issues?**
   - **Question: What steps would 6G take to guarantee sustainability of the environment?**
   - **Answer:** In response, 6G seeks to tackle sustainability and environmental issues by:
     - o **Energy Efficiency:** Reducing overall energy usage by designing more energy-efficient network components and streamlining network operations.
     - o **Green Technologies** refer to the integration of sustainable materials and renewable energy sources into network infrastructure. **E-Waste Management** is the application of techniques for the sustainable recycling and disposal of network equipment and electronic gadgets.

6. **What function will machine learning and AI have in 6G?**
   - **Question: What advantages will artificial intelligence and machine learning offer to 6G networks, and how will they be integrated?**
   - **Answer:** In response, artificial intelligence and machine learning will be crucial to 6G by:
     - o **Network Optimization** is the process of managing traffic, allocating resources dynamically, and improving network performance using AI.
     - o **Predictive Maintenance** lowers maintenance costs and downtime by using machine learning algorithms to anticipate and avoid network faults.
     - o **Autonomous Operations:** Enabling self-organizing networks with the ability to configure and operate themselves on their own using real-time data analysis is known as autonomous operations.

7. **What possible effects might 6G have on society and the economy?**
   - **Question: What impact will 6G have on the economy and society?**
   - **Answer:** The following are some of the social and economic effects of 6G:
     - **Economic Growth:** In order to promote economic growth, new industries, employment opportunities, and sources of income must be established.
     - **Digital Inclusion** is the process of reducing the digital divide by improving access to economic, healthcare, and educational opportunities in underprivileged and distant places through high-speed internet.
     - **Quality of Life:** Enhancing public services, smart cities, and cutting-edge healthcare can all contribute to a higher quality of life.

In summary, the path towards 6G is characterized by aspirational technological objectives that offer noteworthy progressions in connection and advantages for society. It also brings with it a number of difficulties that call for cautious thought and coordinated efforts by businesses, governments, and communities. Stakeholders may successfully negotiate the intricacies of 6G development and deployment by posing pertinent questions and looking for well-informed answers. By doing so, they can make sure that this next-generation technology addresses important problems and maximizes benefits to society.

Table of Figures

Bibliography

1. *Erik Dahlman, Stefan Parkvall, and Johan Sköld (2018);* **"5G NR: The Next Generation Wireless Access Technology"**; *ISBN: 978-0128143230; Publisher: Academic Press*
2. *Chris Johnson* **(2019); "5G New Radio in Bullets";** *ISBN: 978-1696852915; Independently Published*
3. *Anwer Al-Dulaimi, Xianbin Wang, and Chih-Lin I (2018);* **"5G Networks: Fundamental Requirements, Enabling Technologies, and Operations Management";** *ISBN: 978-1119332732; Publisher: Wiley*
4. *Sassan Ahmadi* **(2019); "5G NR: Architecture, Technology, Implementation, and Operation of 3GPP New Radio Standards";** *ISBN: 978-0128134214; Publisher: Academic Press*
5. *Xingqin Lin and Navin Gupta* **(2020); "6G Wireless Communications: Future Technologies and Applications";** *ISBN: 978-3030581988; Publisher: Springer*
6. *Harri Holma, Antti Toskala, and Ari Hämäläinen (2020);* **"6G: The Road to the Future Wireless Technologies 2030";** *ISBN: 978-1119645641; Publisher: Wiley*
7. *Abbas Jamalipour, Yi Qian, and Parag Kulkarni (2021);* **"Towards 6G: A Paradigm Shift in Network Architectures";** *ISBN: 978-1119551690; Publisher: Wiley-IEEE Press*
8. *Yulei Wu, Md Zakirul Alam Bhuiyan, and Lei Shu* **(2021); "6G Mobile Wireless Networks";** *ISBN: 978-3030669129; Publisher: Springer*
9. *Wen Tong and Peiying Zhu* **(2021); "6G: The Next Horizon: From Connected People and Things to Connected Intelligence";** *ISBN: 978-1108842877; Publisher: Cambridge University Press*